# MADE TO
# CRAVE

PARTICIPANT'S GUIDE

## Also by Lysa TerKeurst

*Am I Messing Up My Kids?*

*Becoming More Than a Good Bible Study Girl*

*Becoming More Than a Good Bible Study Girl* video curriculum

*Capture His Heart (for wives)*

*Capture His Heart (for husbands)*

*Leading Women to the Heart of God*

*Living Life on Purpose*

*What Happens When Women Say Yes to God*

*What Happens When Women Walk in Faith*

*Who Holds the Key to Your Heart?*

# MADE TO CRAVE

## PARTICIPANT'S GUIDE

### SATISFYING YOUR DEEPEST DESIRE
### WITH GOD, NOT FOOD

SIX SESSIONS

# LYSA TERKEURST
President of Proverbs 31 Ministries

with Christine M. Anderson

**ZONDERVAN**

**ZONDERVAN**.com/
AUTHOR**TRACKER**
*follow your favorite authors*

ZONDERVAN

*Made to Crave Participant's Guide*
Copyright © 2011 by Lysa TerKeurst

Requests for information should be addressed to:
Zondervan, *Grand Rapids, Michigan 49530*

ISBN 978-0-310-67155-8

Published in association with the literary agency of Fedd & Company, Inc., 9759 Concord Pass, Brentwood, TN 37027.

*Cover design: Curt Diepenhorst*
*Cover photography: Getty Image®*
*Interior design: Beth Shagene*

*Printed in the United States of America*

12 13 14 15 16 17 18 19 20 /DCI/ 32 31 30 29 28 27 26 25 24 23 22 21 20 19 18 17 16

# Contents

*About the Study*      7

*How to Use This Guide*      9

SESSION 1: From Deprivation to Empowerment      11

SESSION 2: From Desperation to Determination      31

SESSION 3: From Guilt to Peace      57

SESSION 4: From Triggers to Truth      81

SESSION 5: From Permissible to Beneficial      105

SESSION 6: From Consumed to Courageous      127

*Bonus* SESSION: Moving the Mountain      149

# About the Study

How many times have you wished and hoped and prayed that maybe, just maybe, *this time* your efforts to eat healthier and lose weight would finally work?

I've wished and hoped and prayed many times and I know how hard it is. I know what it's like to try all the latest and greatest fad diets only to eventually regain all the pounds I worked so hard to shed.

I know what it's like to sit in front of the television when an infomercial promises that this exercise machine or those pills will be the answer to every dieting woe I've ever had. And I know what it's like to sit there wishing the promises were true but knowing in the depths of my heart they're not.

I know what it's like to step on the scale every morning wishing the numbers were different but never having the discipline to make the changes that would result in different numbers. And then even rationalizing, "Well, who cares what I weigh? It's not very Christian to be so vain and want to be thin." But at the same time, I had this nagging feeling that my body wasn't healthy and I knew it needed to be healthy in order to serve God the very best that I could.

All that to say, I understand. I know the tears you cry and the hurt you lug around with the excess weight. But, sweet sister, I do want to give you permission to dare to believe that this time will be different. I have walked this journey I'm inviting you to take and I can tell you with all honesty and integrity, *it works*. Dare to believe that this time it really will be different — and it will.

I'm not going to help you find your *how-to*. I'm not a nutritional expert who's going to tell you what you already know: "Eat less, move more." What I want to do is help you find your *want-to* — that missing link of spiritual and mental motivation that this time really will make the difference. That's what I needed ... and so I set out on a journey through the Bible and prayed a very simple prayer, "God, help me to discover how I can consume food without food consuming me." *Made to Crave* is the answer to that prayer. I have finally found the secret linking God's truth with my eating and weight issues. Not only is it the greatest spiritual journey I've ever been on, but I've also experienced tremendous physical results — and I want that for you too.

I'd love to stay connected with you throughout your *Made to Crave* journey. Be sure to visit *MadetoCrave.org*, where you'll find many additional resources, including downloadable signs and inspirational quotes to keep you motivated and on track. There's even a free "Crave God" magnet you can use to attach the signs and quotes to your fridge! (See the page near the back of this participant's guide for details on how to order your magnet.)

We can also connect on my blog, *www.LysaTerKeurst.com*. Please stop by and post a comment or two. I'd love to know how you're doing and continue walking with you even after the study is done. And I'd love to be that voice of grace on those days when you experience a setback. As my friend Kathrine Lee says, "A setback is really just a setup for a comeback." I love that. I need that. And you will too. So, don't give up.

If you're struggling to believe that this time it really can be different, it's okay. There was a time when I thought I would never overcome my issues with food — that I would always be trapped in a vicious cycle of losing and gaining weight. But I have discovered that what once seemed so impossible to me is more than possible with God. It's an amazing spiritual journey and I can't wait to share it with you.

LYSA TERKEURST

# How to Use This Guide

## Group Size

*Made to Crave* is designed to be experienced in a group setting such as a Bible study, Sunday school class, or any small group gathering. To ensure everyone has enough time to participate in discussions, it is recommended that large groups break up into smaller groups of four to six people each.

Each participant should have her own participant's guide, which includes notes for video segments, directions for activities and discussion questions, as well as a reading plan and personal Bible studies to deepen learning between sessions. Although the study can be fully experienced with just the video and participant's guide, participants are also encouraged to have a copy of the *Made to Crave* book. Reading the book along with the video sessions provides even deeper insights that make the journey richer and more meaningful.

## What's Included

*Made to Crave* includes:

- Six group sessions
- A bonus session for groups that want to extend their study
- Six days of personal study for use between sessions. This includes suggested chapter readings from the *Made to Crave* book and personal Bible studies that track along with the video teaching for group sessions.

## Format Options

*Made to Crave* can be used by groups that meet for one hour or two hours. Each group session can be completed in one hour but includes optional activities and group discussions that expand the material to meet the needs of groups that meet for two hours.

## Timing

The time notations—for example (12 minutes)—indicate the actual time of video segments and the suggested times for each activity or discussion. Adhering to the suggested times will enable you to complete each session in one hour. If you have additional time, you may wish to allow more time for discussion and activities.

Alternate time notations and optional activities for two-hour groups are set off with a gray background. For example:

**Group Discussion:** *From Deprivation to Empowerment* (5 MINUTES)

If your group meets for two hours, allow 10 MINUTES for this discussion.

In this example, one-hour groups allow 5 minutes for the discussion and two-hour groups allow 10 minutes for the discussion.

## Facilitation

Each group should appoint a facilitator who is responsible for starting the video and for keeping track of time during discussions and activities. Facilitators may also read questions aloud and monitor discussions, prompting participants to respond and assuring that everyone has the opportunity to participate.

## Between-Sessions Personal Bible Study

Maximize the impact of the course between sessions with six days of personal study, alternating every other day between reading a chapter in the *Made to Crave* book and then completing a Bible study on the theme of that chapter. Setting aside just twenty to thirty minutes a day for personal study will enable you to complete the book and Bible studies by the end of the course.

# From Deprivation to Empowerment

## Welcome!

Welcome to Session 1 of *Made to Crave*. You're about to embark on a spiritual adventure with great physical benefits! If this is your first time together as a group, take a moment to introduce yourselves to each other before watching the video. Then let's get started!

## Video: *From Deprivation to Empowerment* (20 MINUTES)

As you watch the video, use the outline below to follow along or to take notes on anything that stands out to you.

### Notes

God made you wonderful. (Psalm 139)

Indulge: To take unrestrained pleasure in something.

"Dear friends, I urge you, as aliens and strangers in the world, to abstain from sinful desires, which [wage] war against your soul." (1 Peter 2:11)

*Made to Crave* is not about helping you to find your *how-to*; it's about helping you find your *want-to*.

• How-to = diet programs

• Want-to = the spiritual and mental motivation to make lasting changes

Story of the rich young man. (Matthew 19:16 – 26)

• "If anyone would come after me, he must deny himself and take up his cross and follow me." (Mark 8:34)

• Food isn't bad, but it's a problem when it sabotages you mentally, physically, and spiritually.

• I had to be really honest. The thing I thought about, ran to, took comfort in, found refuge in, turned to and depended on, was food way more than it was Jesus.

This is a spiritual journey that will reap wonderful physical benefits.

If we can look at healthy options and make the healthy choices — and not feel deprived but instead feel empowered — everything will change. It will change us mentally, spiritually, and physically.

*Made to Crave* will help you learn how to feel empowered rather than deprived.

We were made to crave, desire, want greatly, one thing: God, not food.

## Group Discussion: *From Deprivation to Empowerment* (5 MINUTES)

If your group meets for two hours, allow 10 MINUTES for this discussion.

Take a few minutes to talk about what you just watched.

1. What part of the teaching had the most impact on you?

2. What, if anything, did you hear that you didn't expect to hear?

## Group Discussion: *The Vicious Cycle* (10 MINUTES)

If your group meets for two hours, include this discussion as part of your meeting.

1. Lysa describes the vicious cycle she experienced of stepping on the scale every morning, vowing to make healthier choices, giving in to the temptation of unhealthy foods, feeling like a failure, and then starting all over again. How would you describe your experiences of the vicious cycle?

*cont.*

2. Do you ever feel that your struggles with food are unfair? Why or why not?

## Individual Activity: *Assessing My Soul* (5 MINUTES)

Complete this activity on your own.

1. Briefly review the list of statements below and place a checkmark next to those you feel are true for you.

☐ I think about food way too much.

☐ My food choices are often high in fat or sugar.

☐ I feel embarrassed about my weight or appearance.

☐ The thought of changing how I eat makes me feel sad.

☐ I'm reluctant to bring this issue to God.

☐ I have gained and lost weight several times.

☐ I feel defeated and discouraged about issues related to weight or food.

☐ I don't have as much physical energy as I wish I did.

☐ When I need comfort, I turn to food before I turn to God.

☐ I say negative things to myself ("You're so fat," "You're ugly," "You're not capable of getting your act together when it comes to food.")

☐ I'm not sure this is an issue God cares about.

☐ I feel guilty or embarrassed about what I eat or the size of my portions.

☐ I have health concerns that are weight related.

☐ I eat foods typically considered unhealthy fast food several times a week.

☐ I eat for emotional reasons — for comfort, out of boredom, to relieve stress.

☐ I sometimes feel like food is more powerful than I am.

☐ I think I will always struggle with this issue.

☐ I sometimes eat in secret or hide food.

☐ I avoid physical exertion.

☐ When it comes to food and weight, I feel like I am trapped in a vicious cycle with no way out.

2. Based on your responses from the checklist, circle the number below that best describes the degree to which you feel issues with food may be waging war on your soul.

| 1 | 2 | 3 | 4 | 5 | 6 | 7 | 8 | 9 | 10 |
|---|---|---|---|---|---|---|---|---|----|

Issues with food are not waging war on my soul. I am doing this study to gain healthy spiritual insights.

Issues with food are a threat to my soul.

Issues with food are waging war on my soul.

## Group Discussion: *Assessing My Soul* (8 MINUTES)

If your group meets for two hours, allow 15 MINUTES for this discussion.

1. How do you respond to the idea that issues with food or weight can wage war on your soul (1 Peter 2:11)?

2. What insights or surprises did you discover in your self-assessment?

3. If you feel comfortable doing so, share the statement from the Individual Activity checklist that best describes your thoughts or feelings right now. Explain the reasons for your choice.

## Group Discussion: *How's Your Want-To?* (15 MINUTES)

If your group meets for two hours, include this discussion as part of your meeting.

1. In order to eat healthier, we need a how-to (a plan for what to eat), but we also need a want-to — the spiritual and mental motivation to make lasting changes. In previous efforts at weight loss and healthy eating, what ideas, experiences, or relationships

fueled your want-to? In other words, what increased your motivation to make healthy choices?

2. How would you describe your want-to right now? Is your spiritual and mental motivation low, moderate, or high? Describe the reasons for your response.

## Group Discussion: *The Story of the Rich Young Man* (13 MINUTES)

If your group meets for two hours, allow 30 MINUTES for this discussion.

1. Read Matthew 19:16 – 26 and Mark 8:34 aloud. In what ways do you relate the rich young man's struggles with his possessions to your struggles with food?

2. The rich young man is unwilling to deny himself; he doesn't want to feel deprived of his possessions. Lysa had similar feelings about food. She once told God, "You can mess with my pride, You can mess with my anger, You can mess with my disrespectful attitude, but don't mess with my food." How do you respond to the idea of allowing God to "mess with" your food?

3. Jesus asks us to give up being controlled by anything in life that we crave more than we crave Him, which may feel impossible to do. But He also says, "With God, all things are possible." When it comes to your issues with food and healthy eating, what is the one "impossible" thing you want God to make possible for you?

## Group Discussion: *Empowerment* (7 MINUTES)

If your group meets for two hours, allow 15 MINUTES for this discussion.

If we can learn to feel *empowered* rather than *deprived* when we make a healthy choice, everything will change.

1. Imagine you are attending a party with a large buffet. In the process of making healthy choices, you say no to some foods. What kinds of things might you say to yourself that would make you feel deprived because of your choice? For example, "Why am I the only one not eating dessert?"

2. What kinds of things might you say to yourself that would make you feel empowered because of your choice? For example, "I overcame temptation and made a healthy choice!"

3. How hopeful do you feel that you can make this mental switch from feeling deprived to feeling empowered when you make a healthy choice?

**Individual Activity:** *What I Want to Remember* (2 MINUTES)

Complete this activity on your own.

1. Briefly review the outline and any notes you took.

2. In the space below, write down the most significant thing you gained in this session — from the teaching, activities, or discussions.

*What I want to remember from this session ...*

## Closing Prayer

Close your time together with prayer.

## Maximize the Impact

Maximize the impact of this curriculum with six days of personal study between sessions, alternating every other day between reading a chapter of the *Made to Crave* book and then completing a Bible study on the theme of that chapter (see next page). Setting aside just twenty to thirty minutes a day for personal study will enable you to complete the book and Bible studies by the end of the six-session group experience.

# Between-Sessions Personal Bible Study

● DAY 1: **Read and Reflect**

Read the introduction and chapter 1 of *Made to Crave*. If you want to dig a little deeper, use a notepad or journal to work through the personal reflection questions at the end of the chapter. Use the space below to note any insights or questions you want to bring to the next group session.

● DAY 2: **What's Really Going on Here?**

We tend to think of a craving as a weakness, something that compels us to eat something that probably isn't the healthiest choice. But what if our ability to desire — to crave — is something that could draw us closer to God? Would it change the way you think about craving?

> I believe God made us to crave. Now before you think this is some sort of cruel joke by God, let me assure you that the object of our craving was never supposed to be food or other things people find themselves consumed by, such as sex or money or chasing after significance. ... Yes, we were made to crave — long for, want greatly, desire eagerly and beg for — God. Only God. But Satan wants to do everything possible to replace our craving for God with something else.
>
> *Made to Crave*, pages 20 – 21

1. When it comes to food cravings, we tend to go for something sweet or salty, crunchy or soft, cool or warm.

   • How would you describe the kinds of foods you typically eat to satisfy a craving?

- What is it about this kind of food that you enjoy so much? For example, is it the creaminess of ice cream melting on your tongue? Licking spicy seasoning off your fingers? The feeling of abundance represented by a whole bag or box of something?

- How do you feel before, during, and after eating your craving food?

  Before eating, I feel ...

  While I'm eating, I feel ...

  After eating, I feel ...

2. The Bible describes three specific tactics Satan uses to misdirect our desires and lure us away from loving God:

   > Do not love the world or anything in the world. If anyone loves the world, the love of the Father is not in him. For everything in the world—the *cravings* of sinful man, the *lust of his eyes* and the *boasting* of what he has and does—comes not from the Father but from the world. (1 John 2:15–16, emphasis added)

   Using the following list, think back over the last twenty-four hours or the last few days to see if you recognize how you may have been tempted in similar ways.

   - **Craving:** *meeting physical desires outside the will of God.* In what ways were you tempted by unhealthy desires for things such as food, alcohol, drugs, or sex?

- **Lust of the eyes:** *meeting material desires outside the will of God.* In what ways were you tempted by excessive desires for material things — clothing, financial portfolio, appliances, vacation plans, cosmetics, home décor, electronics, etc.?

- **Boasting:** *meeting needs for significance outside the will of God.* In what ways were you tempted by desires to prop up your significance — perhaps by name dropping, exaggerating, feigning humility or other virtues, doing something just because you knew it would be observed by others, etc.?

In what ways was your ability to love God and love others (including yourself) impacted by your response to these temptations?

3. Read Genesis 3:6 and Matthew 4:1 – 11 to see how Satan used these same three tactics with Eve and with Jesus. Note each temptation on the chart below.

| TEMPTATION TACTIC | EVE | JESUS |
|---|---|---|
| Craving | | |
| Lust of the eyes | | |
| Boasting | | |

[Eve] focused only on the object of her obsession. . . . Eve craved what she focused on. We consume what we think about. And what we think about can consume us if we're not careful.

*Made to Crave*, page 23

4. In one sense, we could say that Eve and Jesus had similar responses to their temptations — they both kept a laser-like focus on their desires. The difference between them was what they wanted most of all — what they craved. Eve's cravings displaced God and made Him secondary to her other desires; what mattered most to her was everything the forbidden fruit represented. Jesus' cravings asserted God's supremacy over every other desire, even a legitimate desire for food; what mattered most to Him was the will of God. Do you see why what we crave matters so much?

• Refer back to your responses to question 2. For each temptation you wrote down, how would you describe the craving — what you wanted most of all — behind the temptation?

• How do you feel about this principle — that what we crave matters — when it comes to our food choices?

5. Jesus defeated every temptation — every lie from the enemy — by quoting the truth of God's Word. Truth is powerful. The more saturated we are with truth, the more powerful we'll be in resisting our temptations, whatever form they take. As you begin this healthy eating journey, here is a strengthening truth you can soak in every day:

> But he said to me, "My grace is sufficient for you, for my power is made perfect in weakness" . . . For when I am weak, then I am strong. (2 Corinthians 12:9 – 10)

Your weakness with food does not disqualify you from winning this battle. In fact, it may be your best qualification. You'll have to rely on God completely, and that makes you the perfect candidate for grace.

In the space provided, write a brief prayer that expresses your heart to God as you begin this *Made to Crave* journey. Tell Him your fears and questions, your hopes and desires, your weaknesses and needs. Ask for His grace, all sufficient for you.

> *When I listen to my cravings, I can begin to determine the need I am trying to meet by giving in to the craving. That helps me answer the question, "What is it I need to give to God?"* —MARIETTA T.

## ● DAY 3: **Read and Reflect**

Read chapter 2 of *Made to Crave*. If you want to dig a little deeper, use a notepad or journal to work through the personal reflection questions at the end of the chapter. Use the space below to note any insights or questions you want to bring to the next group session.

## ● DAY 4: **Replacing My Cravings**

When we rely on something, we trust it and depend on it; we have confidence that it won't let us down. If we struggle with food, at some point we have to wrestle with a very raw question: *Is it possible we love and rely on food more than we love and rely on God?*

I had to get honest enough to admit it: I relied on food more than I relied on God. I craved food more than I craved God. Food was my comfort. Food was my reward. Food was my joy. Food was what I turned to in times of stress, sadness, and even in times of happiness.

*Made to Crave, page 29*

1. For each of the items listed below, use the space provided to rate the degree to which you rely on food to give you what you need. Use the following scale:

> 3 = Food is almost always the first thing I rely on.
> 2 = Food is frequently what I rely on.
> 1 = Food is occasionally what I rely on.
> 0 = Food is rarely what I rely on.

_____ When I need *comfort* _____ When I feel *sadness*

_____ When I want a *reward* _____ When I feel *happiness*

_____ When I feel *joy* _____ When I experience *boredom*

_____ When I experience *stress*

Pick one of the items you rated as a 3 or a 2 and circle it. Keep it in mind as you respond to the following questions.

• What behaviors do you typically engage in when turning to food for that reason? For example, if you rely on food for comfort, do you secretly get takeout from a fast food restaurant and eat it in your car, sit down in front of the television with a bag of chips, curl up in your favorite chair with a pan of warm brownies and a fork?

• How do you imagine your behaviors might change if you were able to turn to God at such times? What, specifically, would you do and not do instead?

• What feelings arise when you consider the prospect of *not* relying on food at such times?

I determined to make God, rather than food, my focus. Each time I craved something I knew wasn't part of my plan I used that craving as a prompt to pray. I craved a lot. So, I found myself praying a lot.

*Made to Crave*, pages 29 – 30

2. When we use our cravings as a prompt for prayer, the desires for unhealthy foods that once derailed us become stepping-stones that set us on a new path, straight to God. Here is an example of using a craving as a prompt for prayer:

God, it's 10:00 a.m. and I'm craving again. I want those snack crackers that are literally screaming my name. But instead of reaching for those crackers, I'm praying. I'll be honest, I don't want to pray. I want those crackers. But, instead, I'm going to have a handful of almonds and brick by brick ... prayer by prayer ... lay a path for victory.

Recall a recent craving that derailed you (or refer to your responses to question 1 above). Using this experience as a prompt, write a brief prayer that redirects your craving to God.

3. The psalms are sometimes referred to as the prayer book of the Bible. They not only teach us how to communicate with God, but they also help us to express emotions and experiences that are sometimes hard to put into words. Psalm 5 is the prayer of a man who desperately needs God's help. He is pursued by enemies who lie about and plot against him — much like our enemy, Satan, lies to us and tries to use our cravings against us. Instead of relying on his own wisdom to devise a counterattack, the psalmist pleads his case with God:

Give ear to my words, O LORD, consider my sighing. Listen to my cry for help, my King and my God, for to you I pray. In the morning, O LORD, you hear my voice; in the morning I lay my requests before you and wait in expectation. (Psalm 5:1–3)

- The psalmist asks God to attend to his sighing, a pain so deep he can't even put it into words. In your struggles with food, do you experience pain no words can describe? How does it impact you to know that God can hear even the things for which you have no words?

- The psalmist makes a case for God to act on his behalf. In effect, he says, "Here are all the reasons You had better show up and help me!" If you were to plead your case to God, what are the top two or three reasons you would give to make a case for God to help you with your cravings?

- The psalmist waits in expectation for God to act. This is not a halfhearted or passive kind of waiting. To wait in expectation requires active attention. It means starting each day on a God hunt in which we are alert and on the lookout for every sign of God's activity on our behalf.

  When you reflect on your past efforts at healthy eating, would you say you expected God to help you or did you feel more or less on your own? As you begin this *Made to Crave* journey, how do you feel about the idea of relying fully on God and expecting Him to help you every day?

*Food is my comfort, my friend, and my joy.... Food has become a sort of mini-god in my life. I must change—not my weight or my size, but my heart.*—MARY S.

The psalmist closes his prayer with a beautiful affirmation of how God protects those who take refuge in Him. He says, "You surround them with your shield of love" (Psalm 5:12 NLT). And do you know what the Bible commentaries say about what kind of shield this is? It's a full-body shield—the kind that covers head to toe.* Whatever fears and hurts you carry about your struggles with food, know that you are surrounded this day, and every day, with a shield of God's love that no enemy can penetrate. God has you covered, head to toe.

---

*The International Bible Commentary*, rev. ed., F. F. Bruce, gen. ed. (Grand Rapids: Zondervan, 1986), 561.

## ● DAY 5: **Read and Reflect**

Read chapter 3 of *Made to Crave*. If you want to dig a little deeper, use a note-pad or journal to work through the personal reflection questions at the end of each chapter. Use the space below to note any insights or questions you want to bring to the next group session.

## ● DAY 6: **Getting a Plan**

One of the first steps in developing long-term healthy eating habits is choosing a realistic food plan that works for you. Maybe the word "ugh" just crossed your mind. If so, that's okay. The truth is, this is hard stuff. Doing the work to find the right food plan can be challenging, but it's essential — and worth it.

> I knew I needed a plan. . . . I had lost weight before but I couldn't keep it off for any extended time. My changes were always temporary, therefore my results were also temporary. . . I left the nutritionist's office that day with a plan. Under her supervision and with a weekly weigh-in to hold me accountable, I felt empowered for the first time in a long while.
>
> *Made to Crave*, pages 36, 38

1. Which of the following movie titles best describes your response when you hear the words "food plan"?

   ☐ *Psycho*              ☐ *High Noon*              ☐ *A Time to Kill*
   ☑ *Leap of Faith*       ☑ *Do the Right Thing*     ☐ *Independence Day*
   ☐ *Mission Impossible*  ☐ *Les Miserables*
   ☐ *Life Is Beautiful*   ☐ *Saving Grace*

   Every movie has a beginning, middle, and end. If your past experiences with following a food plan were made into a movie, how would you describe the beginning, middle, and end of your story? (See next page.)

- **Beginning**

  Example: *I feel hopeful as I walk through the grocery store with a cart full of fresh vegetables and other healthy foods.*

- **Middle**

  Example: *I'm at a birthday party and there's nothing here that's okay for me to eat. I feel discouraged and left out. I'm tired of saying no to myself and having to plan all my meals. I want cake—the corner piece with all the extra frosting.*

- **End**

  Example: *I've failed—again. I swear off diets and food plans forever. Roll credits.*

2. How would you respond if a nutritionist were to ask you the following questions:

   - What is your biggest fear about choosing or following a food plan?

   - How can I help you with that fear?

*My problem isn't so much having a plan as sticking to the plan. I hate feeling restricted!* —JANE D.

- What words or phrases would you use to describe the kind of plan you think might be realistic for you over the long term?

3. The book of Proverbs is a wisdom book. It focuses on practical guidance to help God's people make good decisions—and it provides key insights about having a God-honoring plan. As you read through the following verses, underline any words or phrases that stand out to you.

> The plans of the godly are just. (12:5a NLT)

> Refuse good advice and watch your plans fail; take good counsel and watch them succeed. (15:22 MSG)

> Plans succeed through good counsel; don't go to war without wise advice. (20:18 NLT)

> Good planning and hard work lead to prosperity, but hasty shortcuts lead to poverty. (21:5 NLT)

> Commit your actions to the LORD, and your plans will succeed. (16:3 NLT)

- In what ways do these verses challenge you?

- In what ways do these verses encourage you?

- What one piece of wisdom stands out to you as something you might rely on in choosing a healthy eating plan?

This journey will require you to make some tough sacrifices, but I've come to look at this process as embracing healthy choices rather than denying myself. There are lessons to be learned and perspectives to be gained in the season of embracing healthy choices. These will not just be physical lessons. The mental and spiritual lessons gained in this time will be the very thing that will equip you for the long haul.

*Made to Crave*, page 39

4. How do you feel about embarking on this journey to healthier eating? Circle the number below that best describes your response.

| 1 | 2 | 3 | 4 | 5 | 6 | 7 | 8 | 9 | 10 |

| **Discouraged** | **Mixed** | **Empowered** |
|---|---|---|
| I feel like it's all about denying myself. | I know I will have to deny myself, but I also feel hopeful that I can make healthier choices. | I feel like it's all about embracing healthy choices. |

- What does the number you circled tell you about your current perspectives on weight loss and healthy eating?




- How do you hope this healthy eating journey might impact your current perspectives?




As you near the end of week one on this healthy eating adventure, perhaps you're feeling a little bit psycho, miserable, or like it's high noon at the junk food corral. Or maybe you have a sense that this could be your saving grace — you're ready to do the right thing, take a leap of faith, and make decisions that lead to your healthy eating independence day. Wherever you find yourself this day, know that God meets you there. He loves your willingness to explore this tender area of your life and He wants to help you take every step that leads you closer to freedom, closer to empowerment and, most of all, closer to Him.

# From Desperation to Determination

**Group Discussion:** *The Week in Review* (5 MINUTES)

If your group meets for two hours, allow **20 MINUTES** for this discussion.

Welcome to Session 2 of *Made to Crave*. A key part of this healthy eating adventure is sharing your journey with each other. Before watching the video, take some time to talk about your experiences since the last meeting. For example:

- What insights did you discover in the Bible studies or the *Made to Crave* chapters you read?

- What challenges or victories did you experience in applying what you learned in the last session?

- What questions would you like to ask the other members of your group?

**Video:** *From Desperation to Determination* (20 MINUTES)

As you watch the video, use the outline below to follow along or to take notes on anything that stands out to you.

### Notes

When it comes to healthy eating, most people try to fix their how-to first.

• What's missing is the want-to.

• Fixing our want-to provides the foundation that enables us to make lasting changes.

• What is creating the most desperation in our healthy eating journey? That's what we need to fix first.

Desperation needs to be fixed because desperation breeds defeat.

Story of Jacob and Esau. (Genesis 25:27 – 34)

Key question: What temporary pleasure have I wanted so much that I gave up lasting victory?

How to avoid physical desperation:

- Physically, I cannot let myself get to the place where I am so hungry that I think, "I'll do anything. I'm so hungry, I'm about to die!"

- We need to become women who predetermine what we'll eat that day and write it down so that we're held accountable.

How to avoid spiritual desperation:

- Remember who you are. You are a Jesus girl who is absolutely capable of being empowered.

- Use Holy Spirit determination. Let the Holy Spirit speak truth to your brain until it affects your taste buds.

This week's assignment:

- Be women of determination.
- Determine in advance what you will eat.
- Determine who you are spiritually — a child of God who is wholly loved.

## Group Discussion: *From Desperation to Determination* (5 MINUTES)

If your group meets for two hours, allow 10 MINUTES for this discussion.

Take a few minutes to talk about what you just watched.

1. What part of the teaching had the most impact on you?

2. How do you relate your efforts at weight loss and healthy eating to the bucket with the holes in it?

## Individual Activity: *The Hole in My Foundation* (6 MINUTES)

Complete this activity on your own.

1. Use the two charts (below and on the next page) to reflect on your previous efforts to eat healthier or to lose weight. Focus on physical issues (your how-to) in the first chart; focus on emotional and spiritual issues (your want-to) in the second chart.

| PHYSICAL FACTORS THAT LED TO MY DEFEAT | HOW THESE DEFEATS CONTRIBUTED TO MY DESPERATION |
|---|---|
| EXAMPLES: *Lack of meal planning and shopping.* *I stopped making good choices once I reached my goal.* | EXAMPLES: *I had no healthy options when I was hungry.* *I quickly gained back all the weight I'd lost.* |
| | |
| | |
| | |

| EMOTIONAL AND SPIRITUAL FACTORS THAT LED TO MY DEFEAT | HOW THESE DEFEATS CONTRIBUTED TO MY DESPERATION |
|---|---|
| EXAMPLES:<br>*I didn't tell anyone I wanted to change my eating.*<br>*I didn't think my faith had anything to do with my weight.* | EXAMPLES:<br>*I didn't have anyone to support me.*<br>*I felt spiritually powerless and alone.* |
|  |  |
|  |  |
|  |  |

2. Reviewing what you wrote on your charts, what would you say is the biggest hole in your foundation — the thing that has caused the most desperation and so led to repeated defeats in your previous healthy eating efforts?

## Group Discussion: *The Hole in My Foundation* (6 MINUTES)

If your group meets for two hours, allow 15 MINUTES for this discussion.

1. What are some of the physical factors you identified in the Individual Activity?

2. What are some of the emotional and spiritual factors you identified in the Individual Activity?

3. If you feel comfortable, share what you identified as the biggest hole in your foundation—the thing that has caused the most desperation for you. If you can think of an example, briefly describe an experience that illustrates how you have been affected by this defeat.

## Group Discussion: *How Much Do You Weigh ... Spiritually?* (13 MINUTES)

If your group meets for two hours, use this discussion as part of your meeting.

1. What is your response to this statement: "Most of us are overweight physically and underweight spiritually"?

2. We determine physical weight by stepping on a scale. In what ways do you think we might determine how much we weigh spiritually?

3. Using the words listed below, how would you describe your current spiritual condition? Share the reasons for your response.

   • Severely malnourished
   • Moderately malnourished
   • Mildly malnourished
   • Adequately nourished
   • Well nourished

4. In what ways, if any, do you think your spiritual condition may influence your physical condition; for example, in the kinds of foods you choose or how much you eat?

## Group Discussion: *The Story of Jacob and Esau* (10 MINUTES)

If your group meets for two hours, allow **20 MINUTES** for this discussion.

1. Read Genesis 25:27–32 aloud. Esau was in a desperate place, but he added even more drama to his situation by exaggerating. Why do you think he exaggerated?

2. How did Esau's exaggeration of his desperation affect his decision making?

3. What role, if any, has exaggerated thinking played in your defeated attempts to make healthy decisions about food?

4. When Esau traded his birthright for a bowl of stew, he made a short-term decision with painful long-term consequences. How have your short-term decisions with food resulted in painful long-term consequences?

## Individual Activity and Group Discussion: *Determining in Advance What I Will Eat* (16 MINUTES)

If your group meets for two hours, use this activity as part of your meeting.

Allow 16 minutes total — 8 minutes for the individual activity and 8 minutes for the group discussion.

### Individual Activity (8 MINUTES)

Complete this activity on your own.

1. Use the chart on the next page to get a jumpstart on your meal planning and your shopping list. You can finalize your choices and add to your grocery list once you get home. For now, just as a starting point, focus on identifying two or three options you could eat for each meal and for snacks. Then list the items you'll need to add to your grocery list for those meals.

| HEALTHY OPTIONS I COULD EAT FOR THIS MEAL | ITEMS TO ADD TO MY GROCERY LIST |
|---|---|
| **Breakfast** | |
| **Lunch** | |
| **Dinner** | |
| **Snacks** | |

2. Affirm your determination to avoid physical desperation by completing the statements below:

I will determine in advance what I will eat for at least three days. I will review and finalize my menu by:

_____ (DAY AND DATE)

I will go grocery shopping for the healthy options I need and then pre-package them in correct portions by:

_____ (DAY AND DATE)

## Group Discussion (8 MINUTES)

1. What thoughts and emotions were you aware of as you worked on determining in advance what you would eat?

2. What challenges do you anticipate you might face in following through with your plan?

3. How might you rely on the group or other resources to help you with those challenges?

## Partner Activity: Remember Who You Are (6 MINUTES)

1. Pair up with one other person.

2. One person is the listener and the other person is the reader. The listener may want to set down her book and close her eyes. The reader then reads this statement to the listener:

Remember who you are. You are a Jesus girl. You are not a failure. You are not incapable. You are not a loser. You are none of those things. You are a Jesus girl capable of victory. You are absolutely capable of being empowered. God loves you — head to toe. Remember who you are.

3. Allow a moment to let the words sink in. If the listener feels comfortable doing so, she may want to briefly share the word or phrase she heard that is most meaningful to her.

4. Switch roles and repeat steps two and three.

5. After both of you have been the listener and the reader, take a moment to discuss this question: How do you hope remembering who you are will help you this week in your struggles with food?

## Individual Activity: *What I Want to Remember* (2 MINUTES)

Complete this activity on your own.

1. Briefly review the outline and any notes you took.

2. In the space below, write down the most significant thing you gained in this session—from the teaching, activities, or discussions.

*What I want to remember from this session . . .*

## Closing Prayer

Close your time together with prayer.

# Between-Sessions Personal Bible Study

## ● DAY 1: Read and Reflect

Read chapter 4 of *Made to Crave*. If you want to dig a little deeper, use a notepad or journal to work through the personal reflection questions at the end of the chapter. Use the space below to note any insights or questions you want to bring to the next group session.

## ● DAY 2: Friends Don't Let Friends Eat before Thinking

*Accountability.* That's not a word that inspires rejoicing for most of us, especially when it comes to what we eat. But if we can learn to focus on the benefits of accountability, we discover a powerful resource — one that has a huge impact on our ability to make it through difficult days and to sustain long-term changes.

> Thinking it over and knowing I'd have to admit a slip to my friend has helped me walk away from countless bowls of chips and platters of brownies. The temporary pleasure of one brownie would never be worth me having to tell my accountability partners I made the choice to mess up. I made the choice to go back on my commitment ... our commitment. I made the choice to go back to my brokenness and set back all that I've attained. That's a high price for a brownie. Yes, accountability is crucial.
>
> *Made to Crave*, pages 45 – 46

1. Consider these statistics about goals and accountability from the American Society of Training and Development.

   The probability of achieving a goal is . . .

   > 10 percent when you hear an idea
   >
   > 40 percent when you decide you will do it
   >
   > 50 percent when you plan how you will do it

65 percent when you commit to someone else you will do it

95 percent when you have an accountability appointment with the person you've committed to

- What's your response to these statistics? Do they encourage or discourage you? Do they increase or decrease your desire to seek accountability?

- Which percentage would you say best reflects your previous efforts at weight loss and healthy eating, and how does this statistic help you understand the degree of success or failure you experienced?

- If accountability is crucial, what is the biggest challenge you face in making accountability part of your healthy eating plan?

2. Establishing accountability means giving up secrecy and taking responsibility for our food choices. But accountability isn't just about sacrificing; it's also about gaining some things. For example, we gain a companion — someone who can share the journey with us, help us through missteps, and celebrate our progress. Use the charts below and on page 44 to do a brief cost/benefit analysis on secrecy and accountability. In each column, write down two or three costs or benefits.

| WHAT SECRECY HAS COST ME | WHAT ACCOUNTABILITY WILL COST ME |
|---|---|
| EXAMPLE: *I feel alone and sometimes ashamed of having a body that betrays my secrets with food.* | EXAMPLE: *Embarrassment. I will be embarrassed if I have to tell someone I messed up.* |
| | |

| BENEFITS I GET FROM SECRECY | BENEFITS I'LL GET FROM ACCOUNTABILITY |
|---|---|
| EXAMPLE: *I get to eat as much as I want of whatever I want, whenever I want.* | EXAMPLE: *I'll have additional motivation that will help me stick to my plan.* |
| | |

When you review the costs and benefits, what thoughts or emotions come to mind?

3. Wise King Solomon knew the power of accountability. Here's how he described it:

> Two people are better off than one, for they can help each other succeed. If one person falls, the other can reach out and help. But someone who falls alone is in real trouble. Likewise, two people lying close together can keep each other warm. But how can one be warm alone? A person standing alone can be attacked and defeated, but two can stand back-to-back and conquer. Three are even better, for a triple-braided cord is not easily broken. (Ecclesiastes 4:9–12 NLT)

The passage describes three specific situations when two people are better than one: (1) *Help to recover from failure*: "If one person falls, the other can reach out and help." (2) *Comfort and companionship in adverse conditions*: "Two people lying close together can keep each other warm." (3) *Help in defending against attacks*: "Two can stand back-to-back and conquer."

- Complete the following sentences to describe how you hope an accountability partner might help you in each of these ways.

  *Help to recover from failure*. When I fail or have setbacks in my healthy eating efforts, I hope my accountability partner will . . .

*Comfort and companionship in adverse conditions.* When I am feeling insecure or lonely in my healthy eating efforts, I hope my accountability partner will . . .

> *By yourself you're unprotected. With a friend you can face the worst.* —ECCLESIASTES 4:12 MSG

*Help in defending against attacks.* When I feel vulnerable to attacks that threaten my healthy eating efforts, I hope my accountability partner will . . .

- Which of the three kinds of help do you feel is most important to help you maintain your commitment?

Changing our habits and giving up things can make us feel anxious. That's why we must have friends to help us remember that what we're giving up in the short term will help us get what we really want in the long term. If we forget to be self-controlled and alert, we are prime targets for Satan to usher us right away from the new standards we've set in our lives. That's degradation.

*Made to Crave*, page 42

4. A powerful example of how anxiety or desperation can lead to degradation is found in the story of Jacob and Esau in Genesis 25.29 – 34. As you read this brief story in your Bible, pay particular attention to Esau.

- How would you describe Esau's physical condition?

- How did Esau's physical condition impact his decisions?

- Referring back to the kinds of help described in question 3 above, how might a friend have helped to keep Esau from degradation — from making a rash short-term decision with such painful long-term consequences?

A birthright is an inheritance — a future benefit promised to a child. Today's equivalent of trading a birthright for a bowl of stew might be something like trading a million-dollar trust fund for a McDonald's Happy Meal. Crazy! Who in their right mind would do that? Yet, in a depleted state, that's exactly what Esau does — he sacrifices his entire future for just a few moments of physical satisfaction.

> *If you feel that you only have yourself to answer to, failure doesn't seem like such a bad thing. You aren't disappointing anyone if they don't know. It's much more difficult to quit when you have someone to answer to.*
> —MELISSA S.

Millions of dollars don't hang in the balance when we make an unhealthy food choice, but our short-term decisions about food do impact our ability to sustain long-term changes — changes that can make our future with food much healthier than our past. As hard as it might feel to invite accountability into this area of our lives, the future benefits are guaranteed. And there's nothing crazy about that.

## ● DAY 3: Read and Reflect

Read chapter 5 of *Made to Crave*. If you want to dig a little deeper, use a notepad or journal to work through the personal reflection questions at the end of the chapter. Use the space below to note any insights or questions you want to bring to the next group session.

## ● DAY 4: **Made for More**

Having a food plan and an accountability partner prepare us for the physical aspects of healthy eating, but we also need to prepare ourselves spiritually. Spiritual preparation requires a deeper understanding about the relationship between truth and power. When we embrace the truth about who God says we are, we have access to divine power that goes way beyond even our strongest white-knuckle willpower. It's graced power, death-defying power, transformational power — and the Bible says it's ours for the asking.

There typically is a honeymoon phase at the start of a new healthy eating plan and nothing tempts you away from healthy choices. But then you are invited to a party. . . . It is so tempting to give in. Set things in reverse. Pretend it won't matter. But it does matter and not just for the physical or mental setback. It's the denial of a fundamental spiritual truth that will make a healthy eating plan fall apart time and time again. What is this truth? *We were made for more than this.* More than this failure, more than this cycle, more than being ruled by taste buds. We were made for victory.

*Made to Crave,* page 49

1. As children, our identities are defined largely by our families, especially our parents. We know who we are because of who we belong to, and that's often how others know us as well.

   • When you were a child, how do you imagine an adult friend of your family might have referenced your parents in an effort to identify you for someone else? For example:

   *That's Maria. She's Luis and Carmen's daughter. Luis helps out with the student ministry and Carmen runs the food pantry at our church.*

   *That's Lynn. Her parents divorced last year and she doesn't see much of her dad any more.*

   *That's Shandra. She's the youngest of four kids and the only girl in the family. Her parents really have their hands full!*

- What might your statement reveal about how you understood your identity as a child? For example:

  *Maria: I was a "church rat." If the church doors were open, we were there.*

  *Lynn: I was a latchkey kid. I spent a lot of time by myself.*

  *Shandra: I was both the baby in the family and the only girl. Upside: I often got special treatment. Downside: I was the go-to teasing and torture target for my three brothers.*

2. If your identity today is defined primarily by past experiences or difficult circumstances, you're vulnerable to "identity theft." That's what happens when you identify yourself by your circumstances — you lose sight of the person you were made to be. In order to embrace the spiritual truth that you are made for more, it is essential to define your identity not by your circumstances but by who you belong to. The statements below define the truth of your identity as a child of God. As you read each statement, write your name in the space provided.

### The Truth of Who God Says I Am

_____, the forgiven child of God (Romans 3:24)

_____, the set-free child of God (Romans 8:1–2)

_____, the accepted child of God (1 Corinthians 1:2)

_____, the holy child of God (1 Corinthians 1:30)

_____, the made-new child of God (2 Corinthians 5:17)

_____, the loved child of God (Ephesians 1:4)

_____, the close child of God (Ephesians 2:13)

_____, the confident child of God (Ephesians 3:12)

_____, the victorious child of God (Romans 8:37)

- Which of the identity truths above is the hardest for you to believe wholeheartedly? Why do you struggle with this one?

- If you could fully embrace these truths about who God says you are, how do you imagine it might, or might not, influence your food choices each day?

3. In addition to redefining our identity, the truth that we are made for more empowers us with a strength beyond our own. Here's how the apostle Paul describes the incredible power available to us as children of God:

> *I keep asking* that the God of our Lord Jesus Christ, the *glorious Father,* may give you the Spirit of wisdom and revelation, *so that you may know him better.* I pray also *that the eyes of your heart may be enlightened* in order that you may know the hope to which he has called you, the riches of his glorious inheritance in the saints, and his *incomparably great power* for us who believe. (Ephesians 1:17–19, emphasis added)

The emphasized phrases in this passage provide insights to help us better understand and access God's power in every area of life, including in our struggles with food.

**Be persistent: "*I keep asking.*"** Paul is tenacious in repeatedly asking God for wisdom and revelation. When it comes to food choices, why do you think it might be important for you to *repeatedly* ask for God's wisdom and power?

**Embrace a true identity: "*Glorious Father.*"** Glory is sometimes described as a beautiful and radiating light. As children of a glorious Father, we can't partake in anything that diminishes God's light in our lives or negates our true identity. In what ways have your struggles with food negated your true identity? In other words, how have your struggles made you feel like you were made for less (failure) rather than made for more (victory)?

***Find the deeper reason: "So that you may know him better."*** The real reason for grounding ourselves in the truth that we are made for more is not just to stick with a food plan or to lose weight, it is to help us grow closer to God. In what ways does it encourage or discourage you to know that there is a deeper reason for inviting God to help you on this healthy eating journey?

***Discover a hope and power like no other: "That the eyes of your heart may be enlightened."*** Paul prays that God will shed light on our hearts, enabling us to clearly recognize the hope and power available to us. What darkness—failure, discouragement or disillusionment—makes it difficult for you to believe that you have access to God's hope and power?

The truth that you are made for more is a truth you can cultivate. It's a truth you can allow to take root in your heart, a truth you can protect and nurture, a truth that will grow stronger every time you rely on it. Give in to all those temptations? No, thank you, I was made for more. Cheat just this once? No, thank you, I was made for more. Start again next week? No way! I was made for so much more. And truth by truth by truth, you will savor the sweet taste of success.

● DAY 5: **Read and Reflect**

Read chapter 6 of *Made to Crave*. If you want to dig a little deeper, use a note-pad or journal to work through the personal reflection questions at the end of the chapter. Use the space below to note any insights or questions you want to bring to the next group session.

● DAY 6: **Growing Closer to God**

Most of our daily decisions require some kind of trade-off or exchange. For example, we exchange money for goods or services, time and effort for a paycheck, or limited personal time to volunteer for a cause we believe in. We don't expect to get our groceries for free, to get paychecks for doing nothing, or that our cause will advance on its own. In virtually every area of life, we sacrifice something we have in order to gain something we don't. And we do it routinely. So how might this dynamic apply to our spiritual lives? What do we sacrifice in order to gain a closer relationship with God?

> I was once at a conference doing a question-and-answer session when someone asked, "How do you grow close to God?" .... I answered, "By making the choice to deny ourselves something that is permissible but not beneficial. And making this intentional sacrifice for the sole purpose of growing closer to God. After all, Jesus Himself said, 'If anyone would come after me, he must deny himself and take up his cross daily and follow me' [Luke 9:23]."
>
> *Made to Crave*, pages 59–60

1. In the late 1960s, researchers at Stanford University conducted what has come to be called the "marshmallow test." One at a time, four-year-olds were invited into a room and allowed to choose a treat, such as a marshmallow, from a tray filled with goodies. A researcher then offered

the children a choice: they could eat one marshmallow right away or, if they waited just a few minutes while he stepped out of the room, they could have two marshmallows when he returned. Hidden cameras captured the kids' responses. Some children distracted themselves and were able to wait until the researcher returned; some resisted for a minute or two but eventually gave in and ate the marshmallow; and others ate the marshmallow immediately.

> *I've prayed for self-control — right along with patience, peace, and joy — but somehow it never occurred to me that I could work at it. I'll have to chew on that thought some more (pun totally intended)!*
> —BETHANY L.

Thinking back to what you can recall about yourself as a young child, which of the statements below best describes how you think your preschooler self might have responded to the marshmallow test?

☐ Marshmallow? What marshmallow?

☐ I am thinking only happy bunny thoughts — happy marshmallow bunny thoughts.

☐ To eat or not to eat the marshmallow, that is the question.

☐ I can wait, I can wait, I can wait ... *I can't wait!*

☐ Hand over the marshmallow now and no one gets hurt.

Now that you are grown, how would you characterize your typical response when faced with a choice between immediate and delayed gratification?

☐ I'm barely tempted; I almost always choose delayed gratification.

☐ I choose delayed gratification more often than not.

☐ It depends; sometimes I choose immediate gratification and sometimes I choose delayed gratification.

☐ I choose immediate gratification more often than not.

☐ I rarely wait; I almost always choose immediate gratification.

2. Here is a passage about denying yourself that you may be familiar with:

> Whoever wants to be my disciple must deny themselves and take up their cross daily and follow me. For whoever wants to save their life will lose it, but whoever loses their life for me will save it. (Luke 9:23–24 TNIV)

Sometimes familiarity with a passage can diminish its impact; we think we know what it means because we've heard it so many times. To get a fresh take on this passage, read it again from *The Message*:

> Anyone who intends to come with me has to let me lead. You're not in the driver's seat—I am. Don't run from suffering; embrace it. Follow me and I'll show you how. Self-help is no help at all. Self-sacrifice is the way, *my* way, to finding yourself, your true self. (Luke 9:23–25 MSG)

• In what ways do you deny yourself and take up your cross daily in order to follow Christ? In other words, in what ways do you routinely engage in self-sacrifice?

• What, if anything, would you say you have gained from this self-sacrifice?

• What two or three words or phrases come to mind when you consider applying this passage to your struggles with food?

• What would you hope you might gain in exchange for routinely making sacrificial food choices?

> Live with the willingness to walk away when the Holy Spirit nudges you and says, "That food choice is permissible but not beneficial — so don't eat it."
>
> *Made to Crave*, page 61

3. Think back over the last twenty-four hours or the last few days, looking for a moment or two when you felt a nudge of the Holy Spirit in any area of your life.

   • What made you suspect it was the Holy Spirit nudging you?

   • How did you respond? Was it easy or difficult for you to follow God's prompting?

   • Have you ever had the experience of the Holy Spirit nudging you in connection with your food choices? If so, what was that like? If not, how do you hope the Holy Spirit might help you now?

> Don't get distracted by physical food. Don't think physical food can satisfy the longing of your soul. Only Jesus can do this. Our souls were created to crave Him and love others to Him.... [M]any people [are] waiting to hear the message of your calling. Don't get stuck in defeat and held back from it.
>
> *Made to Crave*, page 64

4. Jesus taught that spiritual nourishment is just as important or even more important than physical nourishment:

   My food is to do the will of him who sent me and to finish his work.... I tell you, open your eyes and look at the fields! They are ripe for harvest. (John 4:34 – 35)

A key truth in this passage is that our souls were created to crave God and to love others to Him. That is our calling. When we try to use food to nourish the soul hunger that only God can satisfy, we not only miss our calling, we put distance between ourselves and God.

- Use the chart below to describe your experiences of physical hunger and spiritual hunger.

|  | PHYSICAL HUNGER | SPIRITUAL HUNGER |
|---|---|---|
| What does it feel like? In other words, how do you recognize that you're feeling this kind of hunger? |  |  |
| What unhealthy options do you sometimes choose to feed this hunger? |  |  |
| How do you feel when you've chosen a healthy option to feed this hunger? |  |  |

- What similarities and differences do you notice between physical and spiritual hunger?

- What role, if any, do you feel your struggles with food may have played in your spiritual health and your ability to pursue your calling (to crave God and love others to Him)?

Whenever we feel defeated by an issue, it can make us feel unable to follow God completely.... If we find that certain foods are impossible to walk away from—we can't or won't deny ourselves an unhealthy choice in order to make a healthier choice—then this is a clue we are being ruled by this food on some level. Being ruled by something other than God diminishes our commitment and will make us feel increasingly distant from Him.

*Made to Crave,* pages 63, 65–66

5. In his letter to the Philippians, the apostle Paul includes a telling comment about food:

> For, as I have often told you before and now say again even with tears, many live as enemies of the cross of Christ. Their destiny is destruction, their god is their stomach, and their glory is in their shame. Their mind is on earthly things. (Philippians 3:18–19)

Paul reprimands those whose lives are self-indulgent rather than self-sacrificing. By claiming the benefits of the cross but denying its power in their lives, he says they set the stage for their own destruction.

Complete the following statements:

_____ is an unhealthy food option that would be very difficult, if not impossible, for me to give up.

This food is especially important to me because _____

_____

The thought of potentially giving up this food makes me feel _____

_____

Self-sacrifice is hard, painful, and sometimes costly. The one thing it's not is pointless. Every time you deny yourself something that is permissible but not beneficial, you exchange a momentary pleasure for an eternal gain. Every self-sacrifice in obedience to the nudging of the Holy Spirit positions your heart just that much closer to Christ. And that's a whole lot sweeter than a bag full of marshmallows.

*Just because something is technically legal doesn't mean that it's spiritually appropriate. If I went around doing whatever I thought I could get by with, I'd be a slave to my whims.*
—1 CORINTHIANS 6:12 MSG

# From Guilt to Peace

## Group Discussion: *The Week in Review* (5 MINUTES)

If your group meets for two hours, allow **20 MINUTES** for this discussion.

Welcome to Session 3 of *Made to Crave*. A key part of this healthy eating adventure is sharing your journey with each other. Before watching the video, take some time to talk about your experiences since the last meeting. For example:

- What insights did you discover in the Bible studies or the *Made to Crave* chapters you read?

- What challenges or victories did you experience in applying what you learned in the last session?

- What questions would you like to ask the other members of your group?

## Video: *From Guilt to Peace* (16 MINUTES)

As you watch the video, use the outline below to follow along or to take notes on anything that stands out to you.

### Notes

Nothing tastes as good as peace feels.

Story of flight 1549.

- Big things can often be brought down by small things.

- Our struggles with food are not small things.

I bounced back and forth between feeling deprived when I started a new diet program to feeling guilty when I ate whatever I wanted.

I knew I would be successful one day when I stood on the scale and I felt peace — no matter what the number said.

"But the man who has doubts is condemned if he eats, because his eating is not from faith; and everything that does not come from faith is sin." (Romans 14:23)

Story of the Samaritan woman. (John 4:7 – 38)

" 'My food,' said Jesus, 'is to do the will of him who sent me and to finish his work. Do you not say, "Four months more and then the harvest"? I tell you, open your eyes and look at the fields! They are ripe for harvest.' " (John 4:34–35)

"Let us therefore make every effort to do what leads to peace and to mutual edification. Do not destroy the work of God for the sake of food." (Romans 14:19–20a)

This week's assignment:

- Focus your thoughts on God, not food.
- Open your eyes and look for ways to love others.
- Write the word "peace" on a small piece of paper and place it over the numbers on your bathroom scale. Every time you step on the scale, let the note remind you that your real weight loss goal is peace.
- On another piece of paper, write, "Nothing tastes as good as peace feels." Put this on your refrigerator, your pantry, or wherever you will see it.

We're going to exchange our constant feelings of guilt so we can be women of peace — with our eyes wide open and our hearts not distracted by food.

## Group Discussion: *From Guilt to Peace* (5 MINUTES)

If your group meets for two hours, allow 10 MINUTES for this discussion.

Take a few minutes to talk about what you just watched.

1. What part of the teaching had the most impact on you?

2. Do you think it's possible for you to reach a place where you can feel at peace no matter what the number on the scale is? Why or why not?

## Individual Activity: *My Peace* (3 MINUTES)

Complete this activity on your own.

Take a moment to reflect on your need for peace right now, then complete the sentences below.

1. When it comes to food, weight, and healthy eating, the thing I really want to feel at peace about is ...

2. I find it difficult to experience peace in this area right now because ...

3. If I had peace in this area, the biggest difference in my life would be ...

## Group Discussion: *My Peace* (5 MINUTES)

If your group meets for two hours, allow 11 MINUTES for this discussion.

1. Do the things that make it difficult for you to experience peace tend to be internal (your own thoughts or feelings) or external (circumstances, relationships, etc.)?

2. Which are harder for you to handle — internal challenges to your peace or external challenges to your peace? Why?

## Group Discussion: *The Story of the Samaritan Woman* (15 MINUTES)

If your group meets for two hours, allow 25 MINUTES for this discussion.

1. Read John 4:7–35 aloud. Just as the Samaritan woman didn't seem to understand Jesus' references to living water (John 4:10–15), the disciples didn't seem to understand Jesus' references to food (John 4:31–34). Because they were focused on literal, physical water and food, they missed Jesus' deeper meaning. What factors do you think caused the Samaritan woman to focus on physical water and the disciples to focus on physical food?

2. In order to develop healthy eating habits, we have to pay attention to physical food. But in that process, we also need to stay alert for any deeper truths that Jesus wants to teach us through this journey. As you

think back on the last week or two, how has God used physical food to draw your attention to any deeper truths He wants to teach you?

3. What were the ripe fields the disciples seemed to be blind to? Why do you think the disciples had a hard time seeing the harvest right in front of them (John 4:9, 35)?

4. Prejudice can blind us just as it blinded the disciples. When it comes to issues related to food, body size, and weight loss, what preconceived notions do you think sometimes make it difficult for women to have compassion for each other?

## Individual Activity: *My Compassion* (4 MINUTES)

Complete this activity on your own.

1. Jews did not typically associate with Samaritans (John 4:9), which made it difficult for the disciples to "see" them. Is there a Samaritan in your life right now — someone you find it difficult for whatever reason to spend time with? Write that person's name below.

2. Keeping in mind what you know about this person's life, try looking at him or her through a lens of compassion. What do you see? For example, what hurts or hardships might this person have?

3. In what ways might this person represent a ripe harvest for you—someone who is eager for the friendship or spiritual growth that might result if you could really "see" him or her?

4. What one act of kindness might you do for this person this week?

## Group Discussion: *My Compassion* (5 MINUTES)

If your group meets for two hours, allow 12 MINUTES for this discussion.

1. How difficult was it for you to look at your Samaritan with compassion?

2. How do you feel about the prospect of reaching out in kindness to this person?

3. What role might this person play this week in helping you to redirect your focus away from thinking too much about food?

## Group Discussion: *Freedom Versus Peace* (15 MINUTES)

If your group meets for two hours, use this discussion as part of your meeting.

1. Read Romans 14:19 – 21 aloud. Throughout Romans 14, the apostle Paul affirms the legitimate freedoms strong Christians may enjoy when it comes to food, but not when those freedoms create a spiritual stumbling block for weaker believers (Romans 14:20 – 21). Do you think this is still an issue today? In other words, does the way some Christians eat and relate to food create spiritual stumbling blocks for others?

2. Paul emphasizes the importance of peace and mutual edification over personal freedoms (Romans 14:19). In your church or circle of Christian friends, what do you think it might mean to "make every effort" to do what leads to peace and mutual edification when it comes to food? What efforts would you like others to make? What efforts would you make?

## Individual Activity: *What I Want to Remember* (2 MINUTES)

Complete this activity on your own.

1. Briefly review the outline and any notes you took.

2. In the space below, write down the most significant thing you gained in this session — from the teaching, activities, or discussions.

*What I want to remember from this session . . .*

## Closing Prayer

Close your time together with prayer.

#  Between-Sessions Personal Bible Study

### ● DAY 1: **Read and Reflect**

Read chapter 7 of *Made to Crave*. If you want to dig a little deeper, use a note-pad or journal to work through the personal reflection questions at the end of the chapter. Use the space below to note any insights or questions you want to bring to the next group session.

### ● DAY 2: **I'm Not Defined by the Numbers**

A scale is an excellent tool for determining our weight, but it's a terrible tool for determining our worth. If we want to stick with this healthy eating journey for the long haul, we have to define our worth and our progress by more than the numbers.

> A few years ago, I was in an exercise class when the gal next to me leaned over and started to tell me that she'd spent the weekend with her sister.... She quipped, "I mean I can hardly believe it. I think my sister now weighs like 150 pounds."...
>
> The scandalous weight that horrified my workout friend was the exact number that had greeted me that very morning on my scale.... But for the rest of the class, I couldn't wipe the smile off my face. I so desperately wanted to yell out three glorious words: "I AM FREE!"...
>
> I couldn't put my finger on the exact point at which I finally got past the insecurities that had haunted me for years. But this interaction was living proof I was finally on a healing path.
>
> *Made to Crave*, pages 69, 72

1. If you could be granted one of the following three wishes (see page 66), which would you choose? Use the space below the checklist to describe the reason for your choice.

☐ Every scale you step on for the rest of your life will register your ideal weight.

☐ Every scale you step on for the rest of your life in a doctor's office will register your weight as ten pounds lighter than your actual weight.

☐ Every scale you step on for the rest of your life will register your weight one year into the future.

2. Which of the following gauges do you routinely rely on to assess your body size? Check all that apply.

☐ Weight          ☐ Body Mass Index (BMI)

☐ Inches          ☐ Comments (positive or negative) from others

☐ Clothing size or fit    ☐ Other _____

- Which of these gauges—good or bad—has the greatest power to influence your emotions and sense of self-worth? Circle that gauge and keep it in mind as you complete the activity below.

- Thinking back over your previous or recent efforts to eat healthier, identify two experiences—one negative, one positive—in which this gauge impacted you. Review the example and then use the chart on the following page to describe your experiences.

## Example

| MY EXPERIENCE | IMPACT ON MY EMOTIONS | IMPACT ON MY SELF-WORTH |
|---|---|---|
| **Negative Experience** *I went shopping for jeans. I picked out four pairs in what I thought was my size and none of them fit. I couldn't even zip them up.* | *I walked out of the store and burst into tears. I cried all the way home and felt depressed for days afterward.* | *I kept mentally flogging myself for my failures. One phrase kept running through my mind: "I hate myself."* |
| **Positive Experience** *My sister gave me a cute jacket for my birthday. When I glanced at the size on the tag, I was sure it would be too small, but when I tried it on it fit great.* | *I couldn't stop smiling. Knowing I fit into a smaller size was a better present than the jacket itself.* | *I felt pretty good about myself and enjoyed feeling more confident about my appearance.* |

| MY EXPERIENCE | IMPACT ON MY EMOTIONS | IMPACT ON MY SELF-WORTH |
|---|---|---|
| **Negative Experience** | | |
| **Positive Experience** | | |

- Why do you think this particular gauge has so much influence on your emotions and how you feel about yourself?

Here's another step for growing closer to God that we cannot miss: we grow closer to God as we learn to look and act more and more like Him. The Bible calls this participating in His divine nature.

*Made to Crave*, page 72

3. Here's how the apostle Peter describes what it means to participate in God's divine nature:

His divine power has given us everything we need for life and godliness through our knowledge of him who called us by his own glory and goodness. Through these he has given us his very great and precious promises, so that through them you may participate in the divine nature and escape the corruption in the world caused by evil desires.

For this very reason, make every effort to add to your faith goodness; and to goodness, knowledge; and to knowledge, self-control; *and to self-control, perseverance*; and to perseverance, godliness; and to godli-ness, brotherly kindness; and to brotherly kindness, love. For if you possess these qualities in increasing measure, *they will keep you from being ineffective and unproductive in your knowledge of our Lord Jesus Christ*. (2 Peter 1:3–8, emphasis added)

The emphasized phrases in this passage provide insights about principles we can apply to every area of life, including our struggles with food and identity. Here is a brief summary of those principles:

☐ God's divine power has given us everything we need to experience victory in our struggles.

☐ It is through biblical promises that we find the courage to deny unhealthy desires.

☐ We are to reflect a divine nature — a secure identity in Christ — that helps us escape the corruption of the world and avoid evil desires.

☐ Getting healthy is not just about having faith, goodness, and knowledge. We have to add to that foundation by choosing to be self-controlled and choosing to persevere even when the journey gets really hard.

☐ These qualities keep us from being ineffective and unproductive in our pursuit of healthy eating and, even more importantly, in our pursuit of growing closer to God.

• Which of the above principles resonates most with you? In other words, which surprised you most, convicted you, or impacted you in a strong way? Place a checkmark next to that principle. Why do you resonate with this principle?

• How does this principle shed light on your struggles with food?

*Even though I have not lost any weight since the first week, I have seen progress. It keeps me on track and helps me to believe that I can do this with God's help. He is encouraging me along the way. I sense Him saying, "See, I told you we could do this together."* —JANE D.

- In what ways might this principle help you to feel more secure in your identity in Christ, especially in your healthy eating efforts?

That day in the gym, I could have let the words, "I can hardly believe it. She must weight like 150 pounds" bump around and cause great damage. Instead, I took that comment and held it up to the truths the Holy Spirit was whispering. . . . I had a choice to make. I could feed that comment and let it grow into an identity crusher; or I could see it for what it was, a careless comment. Just like I can make the choice to leave the cookies in the bakery case and the chips on the grocery store shelf, I could make the choice to walk away from that remark.

*Made to Crave*, pages 74 – 75

4. What "identity-crusher" thought or hurtful comment — about your size or weight — bumps around in your heart and causes damage?

What insights do you gain when you scrutinize this thought or comment with these questions:

- Is this thought/comment true?

- Is this thought/comment beneficial?

- Is this thought/comment necessary?

Do you feel you can choose to walk away from this thought or comment in the same way you can choose to walk away from unhealthy foods? Why or why not?

5. Read this statement out loud: "I can step on the scale and accept the numbers for what they are—an indication of how much my body weighs—and not an indication of my worth." Using the scale below, indicate the degree to which you feel this statement is true for you.

1   2   3   4   5   6   7   8   9   10
Not at all true            Somewhat true            Completely true

Based on the number you chose, respond to one of the three questions below.

**If you chose 1–3:** What do you imagine the most significant change in your life might be if you could believe the truth of this statement for yourself?

**If you chose 4–7:** What obstacles or challenges make it difficult for you to wholeheartedly embrace the truth of this statement for yourself right now?

**If you chose 8–10:** What key truth, insight, or experience has helped you to fully believe the truth of this statement for yourself?

Perhaps you've heard the phrase, "Numbers don't lie." Numbers on a scale do tell the truth about how much your body weighs (unless it's the doctor's office scale, which everyone knows lies by at least five pounds). But the numbers on a scale can lead you to believe a lie if you allow them to bump around in your heart and do damage. When you're tempted to let the numbers define your identity or your worth, you can choose to walk away. Your identity is secure in Christ and no scale on the planet could measure how much you're worth to Him.

## ● DAY 3: **Read and Reflect**

Read chapter 8 of *Made to Crave*. If you want to dig a little deeper, use a notepad or journal to work through the personal reflection questions at the end of the chapter. Use the space below to note any insights or questions you want to bring to the next group session.

## ● DAY 4: **Making Peace with the Realities of My Body**

*Peace.* Ah, that's a beautiful word. *Body.* Uh, that's not such a beautiful word for most of us. And we rarely feel anything remotely peaceful when it comes to the realities of our bodies. Dissatisfied, anxious, *unpeaced* might be more like it. But God has another perspective on the body He created just for you; He invites you to try it on for a while, walk around in it, and see how good it feels on the skin you're in.

> I don't know a woman alive who is completely happy with her body. I don't know a woman alive who wakes up one day and says, "I have eaten healthy, I have exercised and, finally, I totally love the way I look." Not me. Probably not you.
>
> *Made to Crave*, page 79

1. In the diagram on the left below, the arrow indicates a level of half full. Using the diagram on the right, draw an arrow to indicate the level of satisfaction or dissatisfaction you have with your body right now. Do you feel like you're on empty (dissatisfied), like you have a full tank (satisfied), or are you somewhere between?

| On Empty | Full Tank |
| DISSATISFIED | SATISFIED |

| On Empty | Full Tank |
| DISSATISFIED | SATISFIED |

- What body part or aspect of your appearance causes you the most dissatisfaction?

- If nothing about your body changed, do you feel it would still be possible for you to change your level of satisfaction with it? Why or why not?

> My friend Karen Ehman is one of my most favorite people to dialogue with about weight loss. . . . On one of her "Weight Loss Wednesday" blog posts she wrote something I found incredibly insightful and profound: *Define your week by obedience, not by a number on the scale.*
>
> *Made to Crave*, pages 80–81

2. How do you respond to the idea of defining your healthy eating progress by obedience rather than by a number on the scale?

3. Karen Ehman made practical her efforts to redefine progress by asking herself the questions listed below. As you review each question and reflect back on your eating over the past week, how would you assess your progress?

| YES | NO | |
| --- | --- | --- |
| ☐ | ☐ | Did I overeat this week on any day? |
| ☐ | ☐ | Did I move more and exercise regularly? |
| ☐ | ☐ | Do I feel lighter than I did at this time last week? |
| ☐ | ☐ | Did I eat in secret or out of anger or frustration? |
| ☐ | ☐ | Did I feel that, at any time, I ran to food instead of to God? |
| ☐ | ☐ | Before I hopped on the scale, did I think I'd had a successful, God-pleasing week? |

If I allowed my brain to park in a place of dissatisfaction about any part of my body, it would give Satan just enough room to move in with his lie that strips me of motivation: "Your body is never going to look the way you want it to look, so why sacrifice so much? Your discipline is in vain." That's why I have to seek the Lord's perspective and . . . "forget not all his benefits."

*Made to Crave*, page 83

4. The psalmist overflows with gratitude and praise for God's benefits — His life-saving forgiveness, healing, redemption, love, and renewal:

> Praise the LORD, O my soul; all my inmost being, praise his holy name. Praise the LORD, O my soul, and forget not all his benefits — who forgives all your sins and heals all your diseases, who redeems your life from the pit and crowns you with love and compassion, who satisfies your desires with good things so that your youth is renewed like the eagle's. (Psalm 103:1 – 5)

- The psalmist speaks to his soul as if it were another person. Following the psalmist's example, what might you tell your forgetful soul to remind it about all of the good things God has done for you?

Forgiveness . . .

Healing . . .

Redemption . . .

Love and compassion

Renewal . . .

> *As difficult as it is to be at peace about the situation after you've stepped on the scale and seen that you've lost next to nothing, obedience is what really matters. If we are obedient, we just have to trust that things will change.* —MELISSA S.

- Referring back to your responses in question 1 (pages 71–72), how does your level of satisfaction or dissatisfaction with your body affect your ability to experience your body as a benefit—a good gift from God?

> The body God has given me is good. It's not perfect nor will it ever be. I still have cellulite. I still have tankles. And though I eat healthy, there are no guarantees—I'm just as susceptible as the next gal to cancer or some other disease. But my body is a gift, a good gift for which I am thankful.
>
> *Made to Crave,* page 82

5. If your brain is parked in a place of dissatisfaction about your body, a healthy dose of gratitude may be just what you need.

- Name one or two ways in which the part of your body that causes you the most dissatisfaction might actually be a blessing.

- Complete the sentences below to identify at least five things about your body for which you are grateful. For example:

*I am grateful for my strong legs because they help me keep up with my toddler.*
*I am grateful for my curly hair because it looks good on me.*
*I am grateful for my healthy lungs because they work perfectly without me ever having to think about them.*

I am grateful for my _____ because . . .


I am grateful for my _____ because . . .


I am grateful for my _____ because . . .

I am grateful for my _____ because . . .


I am grateful for my _____ because . . .


Peace is a good and beautiful thing. Your body — yes, ma'am, *your body* — is a good and beautiful thing. (Please say amen.) And putting those two things together — peace with your body — makes you completely lovely. You are made in the image of God, our loving Creator, whose invitation to you just might be, "C'mon, why don't you give peace a chance?"

## ● DAY 5: **Read and Reflect**

Read chapter 9 of *Made to Crave*. If you want to dig a little deeper, use a notepad or journal to work through the personal reflection questions at the end of the chapter. Use the space below to note any insights or questions you want to bring to the next group session.

## ● DAY 6: **But Exercise Makes Me Want to Cry**

Exercise is good for your hearts . . . both of them — the physical one that beats in your chest and the spiritual one that holds all your love for God and others. On this *Made to Crave* journey toward lasting changes, overcoming resistance and excuses related to exercise is a critical challenge. But we're nearing the end of week three and you're probably eager for a challenge, right? Excellent! It's time to give those hearts of yours a God-honoring workout.

> The many extra pounds that had crept onto my body could easily be justified. After all, I've birthed three children. I even seemed to gain weight with the two we adopted. I'm very busy with them. This is my season of raising kids, not lifting weights. I'm too busy running carpools to run for exercise. But in the quiet of my heart, I wasn't settled.
>
> *Made to Crave*, page 88

1. If you aren't in love with exercise, it's okay to say so. In the space below, give yourself permission to list the biggest reasons why exercise isn't on your top-ten list of super-duper favorite things to do.

If I was honest with myself, my issue was plain and simple — a lack of self-control. I could sugarcoat it and justify it all day long, but the truth was I didn't have a weight problem, I had a spiritual problem. I depended on food for comfort more than I depended on God. And I was simply too lazy to make time to exercise.

Ouch. That truth hurt.

*Made to Crave, pages 88 – 89*

2. What is the truth that hurts behind your reasons for not exercising?

One day, I went out for my version of a run and God clearly spoke to my heart: "Run until you can't take another step. Do it not in your strength but Mine. . . . Don't stop until I tell you to." . . .

As I ran that day, I connected with God on a different level. I experienced what it meant to absolutely require God's faith to see something through. How many times have I claimed to be a woman of faith but rarely lived a life requiring faith? That day, God didn't have me stop until I ran 8.6 miles.

*Made to Crave, pages 89 – 90*

3. In what ways might exercise require you to live a life that absolutely requires faith?

How do you need God to be the strength of your heart as you take your first steps into a new exercise routine?

4. Generally speaking, which item in each of the following paired statements represents your preference:

a. I prefer to be:
   ☐ Indoors
   ☐ Outdoors

b. I prefer to be:
   ☐ Alone
   ☐ With others

c. I prefer:
   ☐ A quiet environment
   ☐ A lively environment

d. I prefer to:
   ☐ Learn things on my own
   ☐ Learn things from an instructor

e. I prefer to:
   ☐ Dip my toe in the water
   ☐ Dive in

f. I prefer to be:
   ☐ Motivated by one small challenge at a time
   ☐ Motivated by one big challenge

g. I prefer:
   ☐ A routine
   ☐ Variety

On the chart on the next page (see example below), use the left column to list the responses you checked for each of the items above. Use the right column to identify two or three forms of exercise or physical activity that honor this preference.

## Example

| MY PREFERENCES | EXERCISE OR PHYSICAL ACTIVITIES THAT HONOR MY PREFERENCES |
|---|---|
| a. *Indoors* | *Walking on a treadmill at the gym*<br>*Taking an exercise class*<br>*Working out at home with an exercise DVD* |
| b. *With others* | *Running with a friend*<br>*Taking an exercise class*<br>*Working out with a coach or trainer* |
| c. *Lively environment* | *Listening to music or an audio book on my iPod*<br>*Taking an exercise class that uses music* |

| MY PREFERENCES | EXERCISE OR PHYSICAL ACTIVITIES THAT HONOR MY PREFERENCES |
|---|---|
| a. | |
| b. | |
| c. | |
| d. | |
| e. | |
| f. | |
| g. | |

As you review your preferences and the exercise ideas that honor your preferences, what physical activities are the best options to try as a starting point?

When it comes to my body, I can't live with divided loyalties. I can either be loyal to honoring the Lord with my body or loyal to my cravings, desires, and many excuses for not exercising.

*Made to Crave*, page 91

5. The journey to healthy eating—and finding that elusive *want to*—requires an undivided heart and a commitment to honoring God with our bodies:

> Teach me your way, O LORD, and I will walk in your truth; give me an undivided heart, that I may fear your name. I will praise you, O LORD my God, with all my heart; I will glorify your name forever. (Psalm 86:11–12)

> Do you not know that your body is a temple of the Holy Spirit, who is in you, whom you have received from God? You are not your own; you were bought with a price. Therefore, honor God with your body. (1 Corinthians 6:19)

- Place an X on the continuum below to describe what your current physical activity levels and attitudes toward exercise reveal about where your loyalty is.

I am loyal to my cravings and my excuses for not exercising.                    I am loyal to honoring God with my body.

- The psalmist asks God to give him an undivided heart. In what ways, specifically, do you want God to help you develop an undivided heart when it comes to honoring Him with your body?

6. Before the Holy Spirit was given to us and our bodies became the temples for God's presence, God was present with his people in a house of worship called a temple. Haggai 1:2–8 describes how God's people started to rebuild the temple following their return from exile in Babylon. As you read this passage in your Bible, consider how this story might apply to honoring God with your body.

| GOD'S PEOPLE IN HAGGAI 1 | ME |
|---|---|
| Results of their halfhearted efforts (verse 1) ... | Results of my halfhearted efforts ... |
| Their excuses for not rebuilding the temple ... | My excuses for not exercising ... |
| What it meant for them to give careful thought to their ways with regard to their temple ... | What it means for me to give careful thought to my ways with regard to my temple ... |

So ... how's your heart — the one that holds all your love for God and others? Feeling a little less divided? A little more open to the idea that God wants to meet you, strengthen you, sustain you in your efforts to honor Him with your body? Or is your heart still pondering, and perhaps a little afraid of the risks it might have to take to make changes? Wherever you are, God knows your heart and He loves the whole package that comes with it. Truly, there's not one inch of your body that the Lord does not love. And isn't that worth celebrating? Maybe with a little dancing, a short jiggy-jog from here to there, some jumping up and down? Go ahead and get moving! It's good for your hearts.

# From Triggers to Truth

## Group Discussion: *The Week in Review* (5 MINUTES)

If your group meets for two hours, allow 20 MINUTES for this discussion.

Welcome to Session 4 of *Made to Crave*. A key part of this healthy eating adventure is sharing your journey with each other. Before watching the video, take some time to talk about your experiences since the last meeting. For example:

- What insights did you discover in the Bible studies or the *Made to Crave* chapters you read?

- What challenges or victories did you experience in applying what you learned in the last session?

- What questions would you like to ask the other members of your group?

## Video: *From Triggers to Truth* (23 MINUTES)

As you watch the video, use the outline below to follow along or to take notes on anything that stands out to you.

### Notes

"You have circled this mountain long enough. Now turn north." (Deuteronomy 2:3 NASB)

Story of Lysa's daughter, Brooke, making a cake.

- Brooke did everything right—except she ignored the directions and pulled the cake out of the oven twenty minutes early.

- The cake caved in because it could not withstand the pressure of an undone center—and neither can we.

If I only fix the outside and don't make sure my center is done, I will not be able to withstand the pressure of my undone center.

If I feel lonely, unhappy, and sad in my bigger pair of jeans, I can still feel lonely, unhappy, and sad in my smaller pair of jeans. That's the curse of the skinny jeans.

Every trigger has to be matched with truth in order for our center, our soul, to become more done—done enough to withstand the triggers of temptation.

When we identify old lies, we need to match them with new truths. For example:

**Old lie:** I need this brownie. It will fill me up with a chocolate high and taste so good.

**New truth:** The thought that this brownie will fill me is a lie. It will taste good for a few seconds or a few minutes and then it will give me that hollow feeling of guilt.

**Favorite verse:** "I pray that you, being rooted and established in love, may have power, together with all the saints, to grasp how wide and long and high and deep is the love of Christ, and to know this love that surpasses knowledge — that you may be filled to the measure of all the fullness of God." (Ephesians 3:17 – 19)

**Old lie:** I am such a failure with this healthy eating thing. Why sacrifice the instant gratification I know this brownie will give me when I'm just going to go back to eating my old ways anyhow?

**New truth:** I am not a failure; I am a lavishly loved child of God. Part of my right as a child of God is to operate in a power beyond myself. The Holy Spirit is God's gift to me and it is possible to use the self-control I have been given.

**Favorite verse:** "How great is the love the Father has lavished on us, that we should be called children of God!" (1 John 3:1)

**Old lie:** God seems so far away and those French fries are right around the corner at the drive-thru.

**New truth:** French fries do not love me and the only lasting thing I get from them is cholesterol and cellulite. They will compromise my life and my health and compound my frustration.

**Favorite verse:** "So is my word that goes out from my mouth: It will not return to me empty, but will accomplish what I desire and achieve the purpose for which I sent it." (Isaiah 55:11)

This week's assignment: Come up with your own old lie and match it with a new truth and a verse from God's Word.

Counting the cost

- Luke 14:28

- What does it take to burn 800 calories?

| | |
|---|---|
| One hour washing windows | 316 calories |
| One hour cooking | 185 calories |
| One hour making beds | 148 calories |
| One hour ironing | 158 calories |
| | 807 calories total |

- When I look at what it takes to burn 800 calories and count the cost, it's not worth it.

- Fill your heart up with practical truth. Know what it's costing you in terms of calories and what it takes to burn that many calories.

## Group Discussion: *From Triggers to Truth* (5 MINUTES)

If your group meets for two hours, allow 10 MINUTES for this discussion.

Take a few minutes to talk about what you just watched.

1. What part of the teaching had the most impact on you?

2. Have you experienced the curse of the skinny jeans — thinking everything in your life would be better if you were thinner? Why do you

think we believe reaching a goal weight has the power to make everything else in our lives better?

## Individual Activity: *How Done Is My Center?* (5 MINUTES)

Complete this activity on your own.

1. How done is your center? In other words, how securely grounded is your soul in truth? Mark an X on the continuum below to indicate your response.

| I am fully raw — like cake batter just poured into the pan. My soul is ungrounded. | | | | | | | | | I am fully baked — like a cake just out of the oven. My soul is well grounded. |
|---|---|---|---|---|---|---|---|---|---|

2. How vulnerable do you feel to your triggers — the thoughts that tempt you to eat things that aren't on your plan? Mark an X on the continuum below to indicate your response.

| I feel vulnerable all the time — I find it nearly impossible to resist my triggers. | | | | | | | | | I rarely feel vulnerable — I almost always resist my triggers. |
|---|---|---|---|---|---|---|---|---|---|

3. Recall a recent trigger that tempted you to eat something that wasn't the best choice for you, then respond to the questions below.

   • What "old lie" went through your mind? For example, "I need this brownie," or "I'll cheat just this once," or "I'm such a failure with this healthy eating thing."

   • How did you respond to the old lie? Try to recall your thought process as specifically as possible. If you resisted, what enabled you to do so? If you gave in, why do you think this trigger is so powerful for you?

## Group Discussion: *How Done Is My Center?* (7 MINUTES)

If your group meets for two hours, allow 15 MINUTES for this discussion.

1. What did you discover when you assessed yourself on the continuums?

2. What old lies did you identify?

3. What did you discover about your thought process when you are dealing with a trigger to eat something that is not a good choice for you?

## Group Activity and Discussion: *Love at the Center* (13 MINUTES)

If your group meets for two hours, allow 25 MINUTES for this activity and discussion.

1. Go around the group and have a different person read aloud each of the passages below and on the next page. As the passages are read, jot down one or two words or phrases that stand out to you. You may wish to read each passage twice to give everyone time to listen and then respond.

   • Psalm 36:7 – 8

   • Psalm 103:17

   • Romans 8:38 – 39

- Ephesians 3:16 – 19

- 1 John 3:1

2. What words or phrases from the question 1 passages stood out most to you? Why?

3. Why do you think truths about God's love might play such a significant role in helping us to become more "done" at the center so we can eat healthier and resist triggers?

## Individual Activity and Group Discussion: *My Old Lies and New Truths* (18 MINUTES)

If your group meets for two hours, use this activity as part of your meeting

Allow 18 minutes total — 8 minutes for the individual activity and 10 minutes for the group discussion.

### Individual Activity (8 MINUTES)

Complete this activity on your own.

1. Briefly review Lysa's examples of old lies and new truths on page 83 and your responses to question 3 on page 85.
2. Use the chart on the next page to identify two or three old lies that function as unhealthy triggers for you, the new truths that counter those lies, and the Bible verse that grounds that truth for you. You may wish to use the verses listed on page 83 or choose your own favorite verses.

| MY OLD LIES | MY NEW TRUTHS | MY FAVORITE VERSE |
|---|---|---|
| EXAMPLE: *I need this brownie. It will fill me up with a chocolate high and taste so good.* | EXAMPLE: *The thought that this brownie will fill me is a lie. It will taste good for a short time and then give me a hollow feeling of guilt.* | EXAMPLE: *"So that Christ may dwell in your hearts through faith ... that you may be filled to the measure of all the fullness of God."* *(Ephesians 3:17 – 19)* |
|  |  |  |
|  |  |  |
|  |  |  |

## Group Discussion (10 MINUTES)

1. What thoughts or emotions were you aware of as you completed the chart?

2. Thinking through your activities for the next day or two, when and where do you think you might face your next triggers?

3. What concerns, if any, do you have about using these new truths and verses to help you overcome your triggers this week? How might you overcome these concerns?

## Individual Activity: *What I Want to Remember* (2 MINUTES)

Complete this activity on your own.

1. Briefly review the outline and any notes you took.

2. In the space below, write down the most significant thing you gained in this session — from the teaching, activities, or discussions.

*What I want to remember from this session . . .*

## Closing Prayer

Close your time together with prayer.

# Between-Sessions Personal Bible Study

## ● DAY 1: Read and Reflect

Read chapter 10 of *Made to Crave*. If you want to dig a little deeper, use a notepad or journal to work through the personal reflection questions at the end of the chapter. Use the space below to note any insights or questions you want to bring to the next group session.

## ● DAY 2: This Isn't Fair

There will always be times we have to wait for something we want, or even say *no* when what we really want to say is *now*. Our heads fill with rationalizations about why we need whatever it is, why this occasion is a special exception, or why a teeny-tiny compromise is okay just this once. At precisely these moments of temptation, God invites us to lean into His strength, to come to Him with our desires, and to grow stronger in the process.

> Satan hit me with a twist that left me momentarily vulnerable and shaky. "But this is a special time, Lysa. And special times deserve an exception to your normal parameters. It's not fair that you have to sacrifice. Look around you. No one else is sacrificing right now.... Special times deserve special exceptions and anything else just isn't fair."
>
> *Made to Crave*, page 102

1. It's sometimes tempting to wish we could exchange our struggles with food for some other kind of struggle or temptation. If you could make an exchange, what kind of temptation do you think you might choose to have instead of your struggles with food? Why does this temptation seem easier or more appealing to you?

2. Recall a recent experience in which you made a food choice you knew was a compromise. To what degree did the rationalization that you deserved an exception or that it wasn't fair to have this food withheld from you influence your choice? Circle the number that best describes your response.

| 1 | 2 | 3 | 4 | 5 |
|---|---|---|---|---|
| Almost no influence | Some influence | A moderate amount of influence | Considerable influence | Overwhelming influence |

If you circled 3 or higher, why do you think this particular rationalization has so much influence on you? If you circled 1 or 2, what other rationalizations exert more influence on you?

> I lowered my head and prayed, "God I am at the end of my strength here. This is the moment I've got to sense Your strength stepping in. The Bible says Your power is made perfect in weakness. This would be a really good time for that truth to be my reality."
>
> *Made to Crave*, page 102

3. Thinking back over the last few days or weeks, identify two experiences — one in which you felt weak and another in which you felt strong. Use the chart on the next page (see example below) to briefly reflect on these experiences and how you typically respond in times of weakness and strength.

## Example

| MY EXPERIENCE | WHEN I AM WEAK | WHEN I AM STRONG |
|---|---|---|
| My strongest emotions … | *When I am weak, my strongest emotions are fear, intimidation, and powerlessness.* | *When I am strong, my strongest emotions are confidence, contentment, and a sense of well-being.* |

| MY EXPERIENCE | WHEN I AM WEAK | WHEN I AM STRONG |
|---|---|---|
| My strongest emotions … | | |
| How I feel about myself … | | |
| How I relate to others … | | |
| How I experience God … | | |

In what ways might your weaknesses have the potential to be strengths and your strengths have the potential to be weaknesses?

What if this battle with food isn't the curse we've always thought it to be? What if it's actually the very thing, if brought under control, that can lead us to a better understanding of God?

*Made to Crave*, page 105

4. The apostle Paul has a surprising perspective on his weaknesses and struggles. Instead of complaining that his difficulties are unfair, he delights in them. He writes:

> But [Jesus] said to me, "My grace is sufficient for you, for my power is made perfect in weakness." Therefore I will boast all the more gladly about my weaknesses, so that Christ's power may rest on me. That is why, for Christ's sake, I delight in weaknesses, in insults, in hardships, in persecutions, in difficulties. For when I am weak, then I am strong. (2 Corinthians 12:9 – 10)

• Jesus doesn't remove Paul's struggles, but He does give Paul a promise: "My grace is sufficient for you, for my power is made perfect in weakness." To better understand this promise, briefly review the definitions for each of the key words listed below.

**Grace:** divine love, favor, or assistance; mercy; loving-kindness

**Sufficient:** enough to meet the needs of a situation; adequate; plenty

**Power:** great or marked ability to do or act; authority; control; strength; influence; supremacy

**Perfect:** being entirely without fault or defect; lacking no essential detail; ideal; complete; just right

**Weakness:** lacking strength; feebleness; frailty; failing; limitation; disadvantage

Using these definitions as a reference, how might you rewrite this verse to make it Jesus' promise specifically for you in your struggles with food?

> *I have begun to see that weakness is an invitation to make Jesus strong in my life. In order to live like that, I must embrace weakness and make the hard choices so that when I am weak, He will be strong.* — LISA S.

- When Paul writes, "so that Christ's power may rest on me," the word he uses for "rest" refers to a structure such as a tent, a tabernacle, or a dwelling.* He seems to be saying that our weaknesses create a unique space in our lives for Christ's power—a dwelling place in which divine strength doesn't merely come and go but actually takes up residence. It's power that moves in, abides, stays. How does this perspective—that Christ's power stays with you in your weakness—affect your view of your struggles with food and healthy eating?

- If you were to thank God for your struggles with food, what "rich treasures" would you say you have discovered on the battlefield?

Our weakness is not in question. The question is: What power will we rely on when we are weak—God's power or the power of our temptations? Every rationalized compromise feeds temptation, making it stronger and giving it more influence over our thoughts and choices. But when we acknowledge our weakness and rely on God's power, we starve temptation. That's why even the small choices matter so much; each one leads us closer to either failure or empowerment. Drawing on God's strength in our weakness, we exchange every compromise for a promise—a much better trade than exchanging one set of temptations for another! And when promise upon promise is built up in our hearts, God's power wraps its arms around our weakness, loving us into a deeper dependence on Him.

> The biggest clue that I'm relying on my own strength is when I give in. I hate to ask for help. I want to have the control and that is part of my problem. —KELLY C.

*New International Dictionary of New Testament Theology, vol. 3, Colin Brown, gen. ed. (Grand Rapids: Zondervan, 1978, 1986), 814.

● DAY 3: **Read and Reflect**

Read chapter 11 of *Made to Crave*. If you want to dig a little deeper, use a notepad or journal to work through the personal reflection questions at the end of the chapter. Use the space below to note any insights or questions you want to bring to the next group session.

● DAY 4: **Stinkin', Rotten, Horrible, No-Good Day**

Life is messy: relational conflicts, flat tires, insufficient funds, difficult children, job loss, unexpected illness, thorny problems with no immediate solution. Most of the time we somehow find a way to hold it all together and keep going. But holding it together can be hard and lonely work. We need a little comfort, a little love, a little reassurance to replenish our depleted emotional reserves. And that's when it's especially hard to say no to the instant gratification of unhealthy foods. In order to sustain long-term changes, we need a strategy that enables us to make good choices on bad days — and that requires filling ourselves full to the brim with God's love.

I think it's worth chatting about being tempted to overeat and make poor choices during times of struggle — those times when you just don't have it in you to deny yourself unhealthy foods. Life is already denying you so much. For heaven's sake, everything you want seems out of reach but these cookies are right here. And you want them. And they will taste good. And no one has the right to say you can't have them. So there.

*Made to Crave*, page 111

1. Which of the following country and western song titles best expresses how you feel when you're having a bad day?

☐ I Don't Know Whether to Come Home or Go Crazy

☐ I'm Gettin' Gray from Being Blue

☐ I'm Just a Bug on the Windshield of Life

☐ If Love Were Oil, I'd Be a Quart Low

☐ If the Jukebox Took Teardrops, I'd Cry All Night Long

☐ If You Don't Leave Me Alone, I'll Go and Find Someone Else Who Will

☐ The Last Word in Lonesome Is "Me"

Which of the adapted song titles below describes how you feel about your favorite junk food when you're having a bad day?

*How ridiculous is it to think that Oreos, Goldfish, cheese and crackers, a glass of sweet iced tea, or a can of Dr. Pepper is going to take away my negative emotions and make me feel happy!* —STEPHANIE G.

☐ I Don't Know Whether to Eat a Box of Cookies or a Bag of Chips

☐ I'm Gettin' Love from Eating Ice Cream

☐ I'm Just a Hungry Bug on the Fast Food of Life

☐ If Love Were Brownies, I'd Make Another Batch

☐ If Chips Took My Pain Away, I'd Eat All Night Long

☐ If You Don't Give Me Those Fries, I'll Find Someone Else Who Will

☐ The Last Word in Comfort Is Chocolate

☐ Other: _____

Taking off my mask means I have to admit that there's a problem and I really don't want to do that. Admitting I have a problem will likely require that I make changes, and changes are hard. . . . It's so much easier to figure out how to get the short-term high of a cookie than it is to get a heart filled up and satisfied with God.

*Made to Crave, page 112*

2. Wearing a mask means pretending we don't have a problem. When it comes to food, what masks do you wear? In other words, what problems with food are you reluctant to admit — to God, to others, or perhaps even to yourself?

What are you afraid will happen if you take off your mask with God and admit your problems in this area?

How has your reluctance to acknowledge these problems affected your ability to resist food temptations or to find the help you need to overcome them?

In a huff one day, I sat down to pray and had absolutely no words. None. I sat there staring blankly. I had no suggestions. I had no solutions. I had nothing but quiet tears and some chocolate smeared across my upper lip. Eventually, God broke through my worn-out heart.

*Made to Crave*, page 113

3. In the hectic chaos of a difficult day, it's easy to pray the kind of prayers that tell God all the ways He could miraculously intervene to change our circumstances: *Dear God, please change these people, those things, and that whole situation. Amen.* It's much harder to be still in God's presence, to listen to Him in silence, and to be willing to pray, *Dear God, please change me. Amen.*

• What is your typical prayer pattern when you are struggling?

- How do you respond to the idea of simply spending time with God in silence and allowing the Holy Spirit to intercede on your behalf (Romans 8:26)? Does this idea intrigue you or scare you?

- If you feel comfortable doing so, spend a few moments with God in silence right now. Set aside your study materials and settle into a comfortable place. If your mind is full of distracting thoughts that make it difficult to be still, bring those concerns to God and ask Him to hold them for you. Then listen, knowing that you are in the presence of a loving God who hears even the prayers for which you have no words. Close your time by thanking God for His presence in your life.

    Use the space below to briefly describe your experience of praying without words. What did you notice about yourself? What do you feel you heard (or did not hear) from God?

4. Making changes that last requires letting go of the lies that deceive us into believing other people or things, including food, can satisfy us. We need to identify these old lies, replace them with the truths of God's love, and anchor them into our hearts with the nourishing promises of Scripture.

    After reviewing the examples of old lies and new truths on page 83, use the following questions to consider your old lies and the new truths with which you can replace them.

    NOTE: If you completed this activity during the group session, you can transfer your answers from page 88 here and reflect on them again, or you may wish to work on replacing another old lie with a new truth.

- **Old Lie.** What old lie or rationalization deceives you into relying on food rather than God for comfort, love, and fulfillment?

- **New Truth.** What new truth about God's love for you exposes the deception of your old lie and helps you to rely on God rather than food as your primary source of comfort, love, and fulfillment?

- **Favorite Verse.** Review the verses listed below. Circle the one that best fits your situation or is most meaningful to you.

    And I pray that you, being rooted and established in love, may have power, together with all the saints, to grasp how wide and long and high and deep is the love of Christ, and to know this love that surpasses knowledge — that you may be filled to the measure of all the fullness of God. (Ephesians 3:17 – 19)

    But from everlasting to everlasting the LORD's love is with those who fear him. (Psalm 103:17)

    For I am convinced that neither death nor life, neither angels nor demons, neither the present nor the future, nor any powers, neither height nor depth, nor anything else in all creation, will be able to separate us from the love of God that is in Christ Jesus our Lord. (Romans 8:38 – 39)

    See, I have placed before you an open door that no one can shut. (Revelation 3:8)

Using your chosen verse as a reference, write a brief prayer to share your heart with God. Tell Him what this truth means to you and express your gratitude for His love.

On a rotten day, food offers a quick and tangible fix. Beating temptation when we're depleted or discouraged requires having a plan—a plan that begins by admitting we have a problem and humbly asking for God's help. The more deeply rooted we are in the truth of God's love, the more empowered we will be. We can say no to old lies and the temptations that deceive us into thinking a sweet or salty indulgence can fill up our hearts. Instead, we can fill our hearts—wide, long, high, and deep with the love of Christ.

### ● DAY 5: **Read and Reflect**

Read chapter 12 of *Made to Crave*. If you want to dig a little deeper, use a notepad or journal to work through the personal reflection questions at the end of the chapter. Use the space below to note any insights or questions you want to bring to the next group session.

### ● DAY 6: **The Curse of the Skinny Jeans**

Reaching a healthy eating goal is definitely a cause for celebration! But achieving a goal weight doesn't guarantee a fairy tale ending in which we walk happily ever after into the rest of our lives. Sad, but true. Attaching our happy to food, skinny jeans, or anything else may bring temporary fulfillment, but we're sure to be disappointed when the fix wears off. Our only hope for lasting fulfillment is attaching our happy to the eternal stability of God's love. Then we can experience something more than mere happiness—a joy that is lasting and complete.

I always thought, *If only I could put on those skinny jeans, my whole world would fall into place and put a permanent smile on my face.*

Yet, here I was, just hours later, falling prey to the same topsy-turvy stuff I used to think wouldn't bother me if only I were smaller. This is the curse of the skinny jeans. My body size is not tied to my happy. If my happy was missing when I was larger, it will still be missing when I get smaller.

*Made to Crave*, page 120

1. What do you imagine life would be like if you were at your ideal weight? Use the chart below to briefly note how you think your life might be different because of weight loss.

| AREA OF LIFE | WHAT IT WOULD BE LIKE IF I WERE AT MY IDEAL WEIGHT |
|---|---|
| Wardrobe | |
| Family relationships | |
| Friendships | |
| Relationship with God | |
| Love life | |
| Work or daily life | |
| Social life | |
| Self-confidence | |
| Other | |

Based on your responses, how would you describe the influence weight has on your outlook on life?

We are taught to remain in God's love so that we won't tie our happy to anything but God. So our joy will be complete. Complete. As in not lacking anything. Complete. As in filled up to the brink with joy no matter if we are wearing our skinny jeans or not. Complete. As in satisfied with a fullness we can't get any other way. Can you imagine how beautiful it would be to live as a complete person?

*Made to Crave*, page 123

2. Jesus tells us how we can remain in God's love so our joy will be complete:

> As the Father has loved me, so have I loved you. Now remain in my love. If you obey my commands, you will remain in my love, just as I have obeyed my Father's commands and remain in his love. I have told you this so that my joy may be in you and that your joy may be complete. My command is this: Love each other as I have loved you. (John 15:9–12)

- Jesus makes a promise: "If you obey my commands, you will remain in my love." How do you understand the relationship between obedience and love in other areas of your life? For example, in relationship with children or in any situation in which you are under the authority of someone else?

- Why do you think Jesus teaches that obedience is the key to remaining in His love?

- To remain means to stay put, to keep on, to stick with it, to persevere. In the context of Jesus' teaching, this suggests that we have a choice — that we can choose *not* to remain in His love. Complete the following two sentences to describe the difference between choosing to remain or not remain in God's love in your healthy eating efforts.

    I know I am remaining in God's love with my food choices when

    _____

    _____

I know I am *not* remaining in God's love with my food choices when

_____

_____

3. The promise of obedience and remaining in Christ's love is that our joy may be complete. Briefly review the words and phrases below that describe the words *joy* and *complete*. Circle any words or phrases that stand out to you or add your own words and phrases to each list.

| **Joy** | **Complete** |
|---|---|
| A deep feeling of contentment | Total |
| The emotion evoked by well-being | Whole |
| Great delight | Absolute |
| Elation | Entire |
| Bliss | Full |
| Blessedness | Lacking nothing |
| Festive gaiety | Finished |
| Rejoicing | Undivided |
| | Intact |
| | Without defect |
| | Perfect |

• Using your circled words as a reference, complete these sentences:
  I recognize joy in my life when ...


  I recognize joy in my relationship with Christ when ...


• If your joy in your relationship with Christ were complete, how do you imagine it might affect your relationship with food? How might it influence the degree to which your weight influences your outlook on life?

Incomplete people are a trigger that make me want to eat. . . . The last thing I want to do when a person throws their incompleteness in my direction is love them. I want to grab a bag of Cheetos and rationalize how much a treat is certainly in order right now. . . .

But what if I dared in that moment to think differently? What if I could be courageous enough to act and react like a complete person?

*Made to Crave*, page 124

4. Incomplete people can be complicated, sensitive, demanding, and messy in their reactions—in short, hard to love. Knowing that we are all incomplete, Jesus commands us to follow His example by loving each other as He has loved us (John 15:12).

   • How would you say Jesus has loved you in your incompleteness? In other words, how specifically have you experienced grace and kindness from the Lord during times when your messiness might have made it hard for others to love you?

   • Think of an incomplete person in your life right now—someone who is sometimes difficult for you to love and may be a trigger that makes you want to eat. What hurt do you imagine might be behind his or her messy behavior?

   • How might you love this person as Christ has loved you? What simple act of kindness might you extend to him or her?

   The ultimate goal of this journey is not merely to eat better or to weigh less, but to crave Jesus and His truths as the ultimate filler of our hearts. That's what breaks the curse of the skinny jeans, or whatever else we may have tied our happy to besides Jesus. Obedience enables us to remain in God's love, and remaining enables us to love others. When we obey, remain, and love, we experience the ultimate reward—joy that is sweet and complete and a bazillion times more rewarding than even the skinniest of skinny jean fantasies.

# From Permissible to Beneficial

## Group Discussion: *The Week in Review* (5 MINUTES)

If your group meets for two hours, allow 20 MINUTES for this discussion.

Welcome to Session 5 of *Made to Crave*. A key part of this healthy eating adventure is sharing your journey with each other. Before watching the video, take some time to talk about your experiences since the last meeting. For example:

- What insights did you discover in the Bible studies or the *Made to Crave* chapters you read?

- What challenges or victories did you experience in applying what you learned in the last session?

- What questions would you like to ask the other members of your group?

**Video:** *From Permissible to Beneficial* (26 MINUTES)

As you watch the video, use the outline below to follow along or to take notes on anything that stands out to you.

## Notes

*Hara hachibu ni isha irazu.* This is a Japanese expression that means, "A stomach eight-tenths full needs no doctor."

Before you partake of food, say to yourself: This is permissible but is it beneficial?

Story of meeting a young man on a plane.

• He was able to fully experience life in a way my adult perceptions sometimes don't allow me to.

• Life is magnificent and yet we diminish it in so many ways.

• God is magnificent and we diminish Him and His truth in so many ways.

This is not a physical journey or a diet.

• It's a spiritual commitment we're making.

- It's a spiritual journey that will have great physical benefits.

Sprint through the Bible. There are magnificent verses God tucked there just for us.

- Genesis 3:6

- Psalm 78:12 – 18

- Ephesians 5:25 – 33

- Philippians 3:18 – 19

- Revelation 2:17

- Psalm 73:26

- Lamentations 3:22 – 24

- Matthew 6:9 – 10

- Deuteronomy 8:3

This week's assignment:

- Identify your new name. For example:

    *Courage*: I am a courageous woman.

    *Victory*: I am a victorious woman.

    *Conqueror*: I am a woman who is more than a conqueror.

- Write your name on something white—a piece of paper, a stone, etc.

We need food to consume, but food is never supposed to consume us.

We live on every word that comes from the mouth of the Lord.

## Group Discussion: *From Permissible to Beneficial* (5 MINUTES)

If your group meets for two hours, allow 10 MINUTES for this discussion.

Take a few minutes to talk about what you just watched.

1. What part of the teaching had the most impact on you?

2. Have you ever thought about food from the perspective that all foods are permissible but not all foods are beneficial? Is this a helpful distinction for you? Why or why not?

**Individual Activity:** *Remembering God's Magnificence* (3 MINUTES)

Complete this activity on your own.

1. When you reflect on God's activity in your life—from birth to the present day—what are the top two or three events or experiences you would point to in order to demonstrate God's magnificence on your behalf? For example, what miracles, graces, or provisions do you attribute to God alone?

2. How did these events or experiences influence your relationship with God at the time?

3. Even though God has provided for you in the past, do you sometimes find it difficult to believe He will continue to provide for your needs now and in the future? Why or why not?

**Group Discussion:** *Remembering God's Magnificence* (7 MINUTES)

If your group meets for two hours, allow 10 MINUTES for this discussion.

1. What magnificent activities of God did you identify in your life?

2. How does God's past activity in your life influence your ability to believe He will provide for your needs now?

## Group Discussion: *Forgetting God's Magnificence* (12 MINUTES)

If your group meets for two hours, allow 25 MINUTES for this discussion.

1. Read Psalm 78:11 – 22 aloud. How would you describe the contrast between God's miracles (verses 12 – 16) and the Israelites' primary reason for doubting and questioning God (verses 18 – 20)?

2. Why do you think food might have been the issue that caused the Israelites to put God to the test?

3. The psalmist summarizes the Israelites' fundamental sins: "they did not believe in God or trust in his deliverance" (verse 22). Despite the magnificent things God had done for them in the past, the Israelites questioned God's ability to provide for them in the present. Why do you think they so quickly forgot God's previous miracles?

4. What parallels, if any, do you recognize between the Israelites and yourself, especially in your struggles with food and healthy eating?

## Partner Activity and Group Discussion: *Sprint through the Bible*

(20 MINUTES)

If your group meets for two hours, use this activity and discussion as part of your meeting.

Allow 20 minutes total — 14 minutes for the partner activity and 6 minutes for the group discussion.

### *Partner Activity* (14 MINUTES)

1. Pair up with one other person.
2. Take turns reading each of the passages listed below. After each passage, briefly discuss what the passage teaches about daily dependence on God or the power of God's truth and how this is significant for you. Note your responses in the space provided.

**Ephesians 5:25 – 33**

What this passage teaches about daily dependence on God or the power of God's truth:

The significance of this passage for my healthy eating adventure:

**Philippians 3:18 – 19**

What this passage teaches about daily dependence on God or the power of God's truth:

The significance of this passage for my healthy eating adventure:

**Revelation 2:17**

What this passage teaches about daily dependence on God or the power of God's truth:

The significance of this passage for my healthy eating adventure:

*cont.*

**Psalm 73:26**

What this passage teaches about daily dependence on God or the power of God's truth:

The significance of this passage for my healthy eating adventure:

**Lamentations 3:22 – 24**

What this passage teaches about daily dependence on God or the power of God's truth:

The significance of this passage for my healthy eating adventure:

**Matthew 6:9 – 10**

What this passage teaches about daily dependence on God or the power of God's truth:

The significance of this passage for my healthy eating adventure:

**Deuteronomy 8:3**

What this passage teaches about daily dependence on God or the power of God's truth:

The significance of this passage for my healthy eating adventure:

## Group Discussion (6 MINUTES)

1. Why do you think it matters so much to God that we depend on Him daily — for our spiritual needs as well as our physical needs?

2. Which passage had the most impact on you? Why?

## Individual Activity: *What I Want to Remember* (2 MINUTES)

Complete this activity on your own.

1. Briefly review the outline and any notes you took.
2. In the space below, write down the most significant thing you gained in this session — from the teaching, activities, or discussions.

*What I want to remember from this session . . .*

## Closing Prayer

Close your time together with prayer.

**NOTE:** In your personal time this week you'll need to read two chapters of the *Made to Crave* book on Day 5 and work through both of those chapters in the study on Day 6. Be sure to allow additional time for reading and study on these days.

# Between-Sessions Personal Bible Study

## ● DAY 1: Read and Reflect

Read chapter 13 of *Made to Crave*. If you want to dig a little deeper, use a notepad or journal to work through the personal reflection questions at the end of the chapter. Use the space below to note any insights or questions you want to bring to the next group session.

## ● DAY 2: Overindulgence

Too much of any good thing is too much. God wants us to live one day at a time, depending on Him to give us just what we need. Whenever we consume too much in order to push down past pain or ward off future anxiety, we fail to rely on God to give us just what we need today to live fully.

> Overindulgence is overindulgence. And limitless indulgence in food always has consequences — it compromises our health, diminishes our energy to pursue our calling, and affects the way we feel about ourselves, just to name a few. It's at this point that we have to admit our issues with food aren't just little things that require us to wear a larger-than-ideal dress size. Eating in excess is a sin.
>
> *Made to Crave*, page 128

1. What do you think would happen in your church if your pastor were to preach a message on gluttony? How would most people respond? Do you think it would lead people to change how they eat?

2. Thinking about the unspoken attitudes and actions in your church or circle of Christian friends, list those that quietly support overindulgence and those that actively encourage moderation and physical health.

- Two or three ways my Christian community supports or overlooks overindulgence as a normal part of life:


- Two or three ways my Christian community encourages moderation and physical health among its members:


- In what ways have you been affected — negatively or positively — by these influences?


3. The psalmist expresses his need for spiritual nourishment — his longing for God — as an intense thirst:

> As the deer pants for streams of water, so my soul pants for you, O God. My soul thirsts for God, for the living God. When can I go and meet with God? (Psalm 42:1 – 2)

> I spread out my hands to you; my soul thirsts for you like a parched land. (Psalm 143:6)

What are you thirsty for from God right now? Do you need a drink of cool water? A word of encouragement? A reminder of who you are in God's sight? Write a simple prayer that expresses just what you need right now.


I don't know about you, but I don't want to spend the next forty years of my life learning this lesson. I want to stop grumbling about my weight, apply this valuable training about God-dependence and portion control, and keep walking toward the victory that can be mine.

*Made to Crave*, page 132

4. As you read Exodus 16 in your Bible, pay particular attention to the ways God meets the needs of His people and how they respond—to His instructions and to His provisions. Then complete the chart below.

| GOD'S PEOPLE IN EXODUS 16 | YOU |
| --- | --- |
| What do the Israelites grumble and complain about (vv. 2-3)? | When it comes to food, what are you tempted to grumble and complain about? |
| How does God respond to the grumbling and complaining (vv. 9, 11-12)? | How do you imagine God responds to your grumbling and complaining? |
| How exactly does God promise to care for the Israelites (vv. 4, 12)? | How has God shown His care for you today? |
| What is the significance of asking the Israelites to gather only what they need for one day at a time (vv. 4, 16-18)? | In what ways can you rely on God to be the perfect portion of what you need today? |
| What does God ask the people to do in response to His provision (vv. 4, 16, 23)? | What might God be asking you to do today in response to the ways He cares for you? |

God knows you inside and out. He knows what you love and what you need. He knows how to take care of you better than you know how to take care of yourself. He also knows what this day holds in store for you — including the unexpected challenges and temptations that will come your way. And He's already out in front of you, walking His way through your day, laying down manna with your name on it, inviting you to dine richly on His love for you, His care for you, His provision for you — a lavish banquet in which God is the full portion of everything you need today.

*My husband and I call it "that snackish feeling." I'm not hungry and don't know exactly what I want, I just want to eat. Anything that's not good for me would work. Thinking of that snackish feeling as the cry of my hungry soul is eye-opening. Instead of opening my refrigerator door and looking for a snack I need to open my Bible and look for God.*
—STEPHANIE G.

## ● DAY 3: **Read and Reflect**

Read chapter 14 of *Made to Crave*. If you want to dig a little deeper, use a notepad or journal to work through the personal reflection questions at the end of the chapter. Use the space below to note any insights or questions you want to bring to the next group session.

## ● DAY 4: **Emotional Emptiness**

Filling a hole with anything we find to shovel into it will never provide a firm foundation on which to build something new. Likewise, filling the void of an old wound with emotional eating and negative thinking won't lead to the new life and lasting changes we've worked so hard to achieve. When it comes to old wounds, we need to learn to park our minds in a new place.

I can remember times when spiritual and emotional emptiness left me vulnerable. The shape of my lack was the absence of a biological father. It was as if someone held up my family photo and excised his form from our lives with laser-like precision.

There we were—my mom, my sister, and me—with this misshapen family and a hole that extended way deeper than an excised photograph.

*Made to Crave*, page 137

1. If you could capture your woundedness in a photo, what would the image show? Just describing the wound you've been seeking to fill and flee may help you to see it as a moment in time and not a defining factor for your life. Describe, draw, or paste your photo in the space below.

One day God surprised me in the most unusual way.... [Although] my dad made no effort to connect with me, a sweet memory of him changed my dark perspective.... [It didn't] solve all the complications of being abandoned by my dad, [but] it gave me a healthy thought to dwell on where he's concerned—one of those good thoughts the Bible tells us to think about: "Whatever is true, whatever is noble, whatever is right, whatever is pure, whatever is lovely, whatever is admirable—if anything is excellent or praiseworthy—think about such things" (Philippians 4:8). I like to call this "parking my mind in a better spot."

*Made to Crave*, pages 139–141

2. Reflecting back on your response to question 1, use Philippians 4:8 and the chart below to see if you can identify some healthy thoughts that might help you to park your mind in a better place.

| MY PAST | MY PRESENT |
|---|---|
| What I know was *true* (authentic) in my past . . . | What I know to be *true* (authentic) in my life now . . . |
| What I know was *noble* in my past . . . | What I know to be *noble* in my life now . . . |
| What I know was *right* in my past . . . | What I know to be *right* in my life right now . . . |
| What I know was *pure* in my past, even if there were impure things too . . . | What I know to be *pure* in my life right now . . . |
| What I know was *lovely* in my past . . . | What I know to be *lovely* in my life right now . . . |
| What I know was *admirable, excellent,* and *praiseworthy* in my past . . . | What I know to be *admirable, excellent,* and *praiseworthy* in my life right now . . . |
| What I want to remember about my past . . . | What I want to hope for in the future . . . |

At some point, I came to the realization that everyone has hurts from the past. And everyone has the choice to either let those past hurts continue to haunt and damage them or to allow forgiveness to pave the way for us to be more compassionate toward others.

*Made to Crave*, page 138

3. What gift of compassion is buried in the emotional wounds of your past? In what ways are you uniquely equipped to understand or be able to help others because you know how they might feel or what they struggle with?

Making long-term changes requires watching what we eat, but it also requires cultivating compassion—for ourselves and for those who may have hurt us in the past. Rather than dwelling on wounds that leave us feeling emotionally empty, we can learn to look for whatever is true, noble, right, pure, lovely, admirable, excellent, and praiseworthy in life. We can choose to fix our minds and hearts on these things, for they are as real as any pain we might recall. We do have a choice on where to park our minds, and God's loving invitation to us is to choose a better place.

**NOTE:** In order to work through every chapter in *Made to Crave* within six sessions, you'll need to read two chapters on Day 5 this week and work through both of those chapters in the study on Day 6. Be sure to allow some additional time for reading and study over the next two days.

## ● DAY 5: **Read and Reflect**

Read chapters 15 and 16 of *Made to Crave*. If you want to dig a little deeper, use a notepad or journal to work through the personal reflection questions at the end of the chapter. Use the space below to note any insights or questions you want to bring to the next group session.

● DAY 6: **The Demon in the Chips Poster *and* Why Diets Don't Work**

Freedom is found in defining healthy boundaries and living each day in a growing relationship with Jesus. Boundaries and discipline keep us safe and enable us to enjoy God's best. Walking closer with Christ changes our healthy eating efforts from a short-term diet to a lifelong spiritual adventure in which we increasingly depend on the Lord to lovingly guide and guard our steps.

> I held the power to determine who would win.
> I held the power.
> Not the chips.
> And the power was to acknowledge that I'm not yet at a place where I can handle just a few chips. My brokenness cannot support that kind of freedom. Therefore, I had to flee. I had to remove myself from the source of temptation and I had to do it immediately.
>
> *Made to Crave*, page 149

1. When it comes to healthy eating, which of the phrases below best describes your response to the word "boundaries"?

   ☐ Don't fence me in                 ☐ I'm free, within limits

   ☐ Safe at last                      ☐ You can't make me

   ☐ Rules are made to be broken       ☐ The cure for what ails

   ☐ Can't touch this … that or the    ☐ Other:
   other thing

   • Use the phrase you checked in a sentence that describes how you feel about boundaries.

   • Example: *Boundaries with food make me feel like a child who stamps her foot and says, "You can't make me!"*

   • What circumstances typically make it most difficult to stay within the boundaries of your food plan? For example, is it when you are tired, attending a social gathering, or feeling overly hungry?

As I drove home, one verse kept coming to mind: "They gave in to their craving ... they put God to the test" (Psalm 106:14).... The desert is a place of deprivation. In a deprived state we are much more likely to give in to things we shouldn't.

*Made to Crave*, page 150

2. Using the chart below, list the unhealthy foods you typically crave when you are in a place of deprivation—feeling tired, upset, or in need. Then describe a benefit from each fruit of the Spirit (Galatians 5:22) that you can enjoy in unlimited quantities at any time. You may want to put a copy of this list on your refrigerator or cupboard to help you "indulge" in the fruit of the Spirit when you feel most vulnerable to temptation.

| FOODS I CRAVE WHEN I AM IN A PLACE OF DEPRIVATION | FRUITS OF THE SPIRIT I CAN INDULGE IN |
|---|---|
| EXAMPLE: *Ice cream* | Love is ... *knowing God smiles when thinking of me.* |
| EXAMPLE: *Cookies and brownies* | Joy is ... *believing that even small decisions lead me closer to empowerment and lasting changes.* |
| EXAMPLE: *Cheez-Its* | Peace is ... *measuring my progress by obedience rather than the numbers on the scale.* |
| | Love is ... |
| | Joy is ... |
| | Peace is ... |
| | Patience is ... |
| | Kindness is ... |
| | Goodness is ... |
| | Faithfulness is ... |
| | Gentleness is ... |
| | Self-control is ... |

> We must embrace the boundaries of the healthy eating plan we choose. We must see them as parameters that define our freedom ... And we must affirm these boundaries as gifts from a God who cares about our health, not restrictive fences meant to keep us from enjoying life. Vulnerable, broken taste buds can't handle certain kinds of freedom. So, boundaries keep us safe, not restricted.
>
> *Made to Crave*, pages 150–151

3. Review the list of healthy boundaries below. Use the space provided to write "restriction" or "safety" next to each statement, indicating whether you experience that boundary more like a punishing restriction or more like a hedge of safety.

_____ God has given me power over my food choices. I hold the power — not the food. So, if I'm not supposed to eat it, I won't put it in my mouth.

_____ I was made for more than being stuck in a vicious cycle of defeat. I am not made to be a victim of my poor choices. I was made to be a victorious child of God.

_____ When I am struggling and considering a compromise, I will force myself to think past this moment and ask myself, "How will I feel about this choice tomorrow morning?"

_____ If I am in a situation where the temptation is overwhelming, I will have to choose to either remove the temptation or remove myself from the situation.

_____ When I am invited to a party or another special occasion rolls around, I can find ways to celebrate that don't involve blowing my healthy eating plan.

_____ Struggling with my weight isn't God's mean curse for me. Being overweight is an outside indication that internal changes are needed for my body to function properly and for me to feel well.

_____ I have these boundaries in place not for restriction but to define the parameters of my freedom. My brokenness can't handle more freedom than this right now. And I'm good with that.

*cont.*

- Circle one or two of the boundaries you listed as "safety." Thinking back to a recent occasion on which you chose to eat something you knew wasn't the best choice for you, how might the boundary or boundaries you circled have helped you to make a better choice?

- Thinking ahead to the challenges you might face in the next day or two, how might you use the boundary or boundaries you circled to keep yourself safe from temptation and poor choices?

We aren't to flee food. We need food. But we are to flee the control food can have over our lives. If we flee from the pattern of idolizing food and stop depending on food to make us feel emotionally better, we will be able to more clearly see the way out God promises to provide when we are tempted.

*Made to Crave*, page 159

4. Here is a biblical perspective on temptation from the apostle Paul:

> If you think you are standing strong, be careful not to fall. The temptations in your life are no different from what others experience. And God is faithful. He will not allow the temptation to be more than you can stand. When you are tempted, he will show you a way out so that you can endure. So, my dear friends, flee from the worship of idols. (1 Corinthians 10:12–14 NLT)

- Thinking back on a recent or past occasion in which you consumed an ill-sized portion or made an unhealthy food choice, can you now see a way or ways out that God provided?

- Looking ahead to the next time you will be tempted to eat too much or to make an unhealthy choice, use the phrases from 1 Corinthians 10 on the next page to describe how you will rely on God to help you.

God is faithful ...

God will not allow the temptation to be more than I can stand ...

God will show me a way out ...

I will flee ...

I'm not on a diet. I'm on a journey with Jesus to learn the fine art of self-discipline for the purpose of holiness.... Deciding ahead of time what I will and will not eat is a crucial part of this journey.

*Made to Crave*, page 158

5. You are on a journey with Jesus to learn the fine art of self-discipline for the purpose of holiness. Take a few moments to decide now how you will make healthy, holy choices today for your body, mind, and spirit. Use the practices suggested on the chart below or identify your own practices.

| MY BODY PLAN<br>What I Will Eat | MY MIND PLAN<br>Where I Will Park My Mind | MY SPIRIT PLAN<br>How I Will Connect with God |
|---|---|---|
| **Morning:** Breakfast and healthy mid-morning snack | The empowering Scripture verse or healthy eating boundary I will carry with me throughout the morning ... | My Morning Prayer |

*cont.*

| MY BODY PLAN<br>What I Will Eat | MY MIND PLAN<br>Where I Will Park My Mind | MY SPIRIT PLAN<br>How I Will Connect with God |
|---|---|---|
| **Midday:** Lunch and healthy afternoon snack | As I eat lunch, I will review the morning and write down two or three things for which I am grateful. I will park my mind on those things this afternoon. | My Midday Prayer |
| **Evening:** Dinner and healthy evening snack | After dinner, I will review my day and write down the ways I experienced God's protection, care, or leading. I will park my mind on those things as I lie down to sleep. | My Evening Prayer |

God created us and told us to be faithful with the bodies we've been given. The Holy Spirit empowers us to make lasting change. And Jesus lovingly guides and guards us as we walk with Him, moment by moment, choice by choice, day by day.

*Made to Crave*, page 163

Take a deep breath in and let it out slowly. Today's study is done. Before moving on with the rest of your day or evening, pause a moment to briefly think through what the next twenty-four hours holds for you. Perhaps you will be caring for children, working at home or at a job, meeting with friends or colleagues, watching television, or going to a movie. Whatever the coming day includes, for a brief moment, close your eyes and imagine that Jesus is physically present with you as you walk through your day. Notice what impact His presence has on you — how you feel, the decisions you make, the questions you ask, etc. As you imagine reaching the end of your day, close your time of reflection with a brief prayer. Tell Jesus what you need from Him and thank Him in advance for all the ways He will guide and guard you in the day ahead.

# From Consumed to Courageous

## Group Discussion: *The Week in Review* (5 MINUTES)

If your group meets for two hours, allow 20 MINUTES for this discussion.

Welcome to Session 6 of *Made to Crave*. A key part of this healthy eating adventure is sharing your journey with each other. Before watching the video, take some time to talk about your experiences since the last meeting. For example:

- What insights did you discover in the Bible studies or the *Made to Crave* chapters you read?

- What challenges or victories did you experience in applying what you learned in the last session?

- What questions would you like to ask the other members of your group?

## Video: *From Consumed to Courageous* (27 MINUTES)

As you watch the video, use the outline below to follow along or to take notes on anything that stands out to you.

### Notes

We have to make the courageous choice not to be consumed with food.

Story of boys in a Liberian orphanage.

What would happen if we decided to stand in our pantries with no one else looking and make a courageous choice?

Courage is a woman who says, "God, thank You for letting me have this issue because without it, I would never have discovered all these beautiful truths."

"May God himself, the God of peace, sanctify you through and through. May your whole spirit, soul and body be kept blameless at the coming of our Lord Jesus Christ. The one who calls you is faithful and he will do it." (1 Thessalonians 5:23 – 24)

God will give you the power to become more courageous than you ever knew you could be.

We need to mark this journey with a spiritual marker.

- Deuteronomy 6:8 – 9



- Joshua 4:1 – 7



- Story of Lysa's sister. (Jeremiah 29:11)



- Assignment: Come up with a spiritual marker.
  *Examples:*
  Frame a word that means the most to you.
  Write the word "peace" on your scale.
  Write your new name on a white stone.



You are a courageous woman capable of craving God and God alone.



## Group Discussion: *From Consumed to Courageous* (5 MINUTES)

If your group meets for two hours, allow 10 MINUTES for this discussion.

Take a few minutes to talk about what you just watched.

1. What part of the teaching had the most impact on you?

2. How do you relate the story about the boys' decision to practice singing with no promise of recognition to your own decisions about healthy eating?

## Individual Activity: *For Good* (3 MINUTES)

Complete this activity on your own.

1. Struggling with food sometimes seems unfair, but God can take the most unlikely things in our lives and use them for good. Thinking back on your experiences through the last five sessions, list three to five good things you have learned or experienced precisely because food is your issue.

2. Complete the sentences below.

   I am grateful for my struggles with food because ...

   I can be less consumed with food and more courageous on my healthy eating journey because ...

## Group Discussion: *For Good* (5 MINUTES)

If your group meets for two hours, allow 10 MINUTES for this discussion.

1. What are some of the good things you have learned or experienced because food is your issue?

2. In what ways, if any, does it help you to think of your struggles with food as something God can use for good rather than as something that's unfair?

## Group Discussion: *Peace, Purpose, Courage* (13 MINUTES)

If your group meets for two hours, allow 25 MINUTES for this discussion.

1. Read 1 Thessalonians 5:23–24 aloud. The apostle Paul emphasizes the attribute of divine peace in referring to God. Briefly review the two lists below. On the "Peace Is Not" list, which two or three words best describe your past struggles with food? On the "Peace Is" list, which two or three words best describe what you hope the God of peace will help you to experience as you continue your healthy eating journey?

| Peace Is Not ... | Peace Is ... |
| --- | --- |
| Disorder | Harmony |
| Chaos | Well-being |
| Disarray | Agreement |
| Confusion | Unity |
| Mess | Order |
| Turmoil | Rest |
| Unrest | Tranquility |
| Complaint | Quiet |
| Protest | Serenity |
| Grumbling | Stability |

2. To sanctify something means to bless it, make it holy, purify it, and set it apart for a special purpose — a divine purpose. This work of sanctification is something that God does for us (verse 23). If you allowed God to sanctify your healthy eating journey — to bless it, make it holy, purify it — how do you imagine He might use it for a divine purpose?

3. What courage—and encouragement—do you take from verse 24, "The one who calls you is faithful and he will do it"?

## Partner Activity and Group Discussion: *My Spiritual Marker*
(22 MINUTES)

If your group meets for two hours, use this activity and discussion as part of your meeting. Allow 22 minutes total — 10 minutes for the partner activity and 12 minutes for the group discussion.

### *Partner Activity* (10 MINUTES)

Read Joshua 4:1 – 7 aloud. Discuss the questions that follow and note your observations in the space provided.

1. What words and phrases characterize the physical attributes of the memorial (its size, complexity, degree of refinement, etc.)?

2. In what ways is the memorial symbolic of the event it commemorates?

3. How would you describe the purpose of the memorial?

### *Group Discussion* (12 MINUTES)

1. Based on your observations of Joshua 4:1 – 7, how would you describe the characteristics and purpose of an effective spiritual marker?

2. Whon you think about how God has been at work in your life through *Made to Crave*, what is the key experience or insight you want to commemorate?

3. What kinds of objects or images come to mind as possibilities for your spiritual marker?

## Individual Activity: *What I Want to Remember* (2 MINUTES)

Complete this activity on your own.

1. Briefly review the outline and any notes you took.

2. In the space below, write down the most significant thing you gained in this session — from the teaching, activities, or discussions.

*What I want to remember from this session . . .*

## Closing Prayer

Close your time together with prayer.

# Between-Sessions Personal Bible Study

### ● DAY 1: Read and Reflect

Read chapter 17 of *Made to Crave*. If you want to dig a little deeper, use a notepad or journal to work through the personal reflection questions at the end of the chapter. Use the space below to note any insights or questions you want to bring to the next group session.

### ● DAY 2: The Very Next Choice We Make

The decision to make sacrificial food choices is more than just a physical decision. It's a spiritual one as well. The challenge is that it's not a one-time decision; it's a decision we make again and again. Every choice matters — especially the very next choice we make.

> God wants us to step back and let the emptying process have its way until we start desiring a holier approach to life. The gap between our frail discipline and God's available strength is bridged with nothing but a simple choice on our part to pursue this holiness.
>
> *Made to Crave*, page 168

1. As you consider your recent experiences on this healthy eating adventure, where would you say you are right now? Are you standing mostly on your own self-discipline? In the process of making daily choices to pursue holiness? Standing fully on God's available strength? On the illustration on the next page, draw an "X" and write "I am here" to indicate where you feel you are on your journey.

What thoughts or feelings come to mind when you look at where you are on the illustration? For example, do you feel encouraged and hopeful, discouraged and fearful? Why?

Even when we stand on the scale and see our goal weight staring back at us, we're always just one choice away from reversing all the progress we've made. I'm not saying victory isn't possible. But victory isn't a place we arrive at and then relax. Victory is when we pick something healthy over something not beneficial for us. And we maintain our victories with each next choice.

*Made to Crave*, page 170

2. When you imagine achieving victory in your struggles with food, what kinds of things do you hope will be true for you?

How do you respond to the idea that victory isn't a final destination but a lifelong process of consistently picking something healthy over something not beneficial?

Making the connection between my daily disciplines with food and my desire to pursue holiness is crucial. Holiness doesn't just deal with my spiritual life; it very much deals with my physical life as well.

*Made to Crave*, page 169

3. Holiness is about purity; it means to be set apart for a noble use. In his writings, the apostle Paul affirms the need for holiness in every aspect of our lives.

> Since we have these promises, dear friends, let us purify ourselves from everything that contaminates body and spirit, perfecting holiness out of reverence for God. (2 Corinthians 7:1)

> You were taught, with regard to your former way of life, to put off your old self, which is being corrupted by its deceitful desires; to be made new in the attitude of your minds; and to put on the new self, created to be like God in true righteousness and holiness. (Ephesians 4:22 – 24)

> I put this in human terms because you are weak in your natural selves. Just as you used to offer the parts of your body in slavery to impurity and to ever-increasing wickedness, so now offer them in slavery to righteousness leading to holiness. (Romans 6:19)

• Circle the passage above that speaks to you most clearly about your own need for holiness. What invitation might God be extending to you through this passage?

• There are many aspects of our physical lives. When you consider each of the aspects listed below, what might it mean for you to pursue holiness — to purify your body in this area and set it apart for a noble use?

Food and nutrition:

Exercise:

Rest:

Sexuality:

Cleanliness:

Overall health:

> The very next choice I make is a crucial one. Literally, it will determine if I am walking the path of victory or compromise. One wise choice can lead to two, can lead to three, can lead to a thousand, can lead to the sweet place of utter dependence on God and lasting discipline.
>
> *Made to Crave*, page 175

4. What are the next two or three choices you will likely need to make about food (for example, what to eat for a meal or snack, what portion size to eat, whether or not to eat something you hadn't planned on, etc.)? List your upcoming choices below and on the next page, and then describe what it would mean to "walk the path of victory" for each choice.

**Example**

Choice 1: *What will I order from the menu during my business lunch today?*

Path of victory: *I can use the Internet to look up the nutritional information for the restaurant so I know in advance what the healthiest options are.*

• Choice 1:

Path of victory:

> *Today at the grocery store I just kept hearing the words "next choice" and I found that I made better choices and am positioning myself to do this the right way.* —CARRIE G.

• Choice 2:

Path of victory:

> *In thirty years of yo-yo dieting I have never been as serious as I am now about changing my eating habits. I'm buying so many fruits and vegetables that my husband thinks I am unsettled!* —KELLY W.

• Choice 3:

Path of victory:

5. As you think back on your experiences on this *Made to Crave* journey, do you recognize ways in which God has rewritten the desires of your heart? When it comes to your desires — specifically related to God and food — in what ways would you say your perspectives have changed since session one?

A choice can be many things — a privilege, an opportunity, a blessing, a responsibility. When it comes to struggles with food, a choice can also be an occasion to say "I love You" to God. As you make your next food choice, you might pray something like this:

> *Lord, I love You so much I'm choosing holiness for my body with this decision about food. It may not be a huge decision in the grand scheme of things but I want every choice I make to demonstrate my love for You and my longing for holiness. Amen.*

● DAY 3: **Read and Reflect**

Read chapter 18 of *Made to Crave*. If you want to dig a little deeper, use a notepad or journal to work through the personal reflection questions at the end of the chapter. Use the space below to note any insights or questions you want to bring to the next group session.

● DAY 4: **Things Lost, Better Things Gained**

The *Made to Crave* adventure is all about gains and losses — gaining empowerment, confidence, holiness; losing defeat, failure, compromise. And of course there are the sacrificial food choices that get tallied with the losses as well. We expect those losses to sting, and they do at first, but the farther along we get on the journey, the more we begin to realize that every intentional loss and sacrifice returns a tenfold blessing — a blessing we couldn't experience any other way.

> What if this whole journey of getting healthy could be more about what we're gaining than what we're losing? In the midst of losing chips and chocolate, there are things to be gained. Things that unleash my weighted down soul, reinflate my defeated attitude, and set loose a hope that maybe, just maybe, I *can*.
>
> *Made to Crave*, page 179

1. Use the continuums below to assess yourself. Place an X on the continuums to describe your perspective right now. Then answer the related questions on the next page.

| I am focused on the things I'm losing and all the foods I can't have. | I am focused on all the things I'm gaining. |

| I can't. | I can. |

| I feel defeated. | I feel empowered. |

- If you placed yourself on the left half of any continuums, what obstacle or issue can you identify that is holding you back?

  Who is someone — a friend, member of your group, professional counselor, or healthcare provider — you could talk to that might be able to help you with this issue?

- If you placed yourself on the right half of any continuums, what insights or practices can you identify that have been key to your progress? How might you rely on these things even more to help you sustain your progress?

> Today at lunch I threw away most of the sweet potato biscuit that came on the side with my salad entrée.... And while tossing it, I smiled and said to myself, "This isn't a sign that I'm being deprived. This isn't a trigger for me to pout and say it's not fair. This is a sacrifice I'm willing to make in order to gain something so much greater than the rest of this biscuit. This is the most empowering thing I can do in this moment!" I can. So, I did.
>
> *Made to Crave*, page 180

2. The idea of giving up in order to gain is a biblical one. Jesus said, "If any of you wants to be my follower, you must turn from your selfish ways, take up your cross, and follow me. If you try to hang on to your life, you will lose it. But if you give up your life for my sake, you will save it" (Matthew 16:24 – 25 NLT).

   - What has been the most difficult thing you feel you've given up on this journey?

- What would you say you have gained or learned in the process of sacrificing that thing?

- What impact has this sacrifice had on your relationship with Christ?

3. The apostle Paul has a very clear perspective on gains and losses:

> "Everything is permissible for me" — but not everything is beneficial. "Everything is permissible for me" — but I will not be mastered by anything. "Food for the stomach and the stomach for food" — but God will destroy them both. (1 Corinthians 6:12 – 13a)

> Yes, everything else is worthless when compared with the infinite value of knowing Christ Jesus my Lord. For his sake I have discarded everything else, counting it all garbage, so that I could gain Christ and become one with him. (Philippians 3:7 – 9a NLT)

- In the passage from 1 Corinthians 6, Paul acknowledges three statements of truth and then puts a twist on them by declaring even deeper truths. How would you state these deeper truths in your own words?

**Truth:** Everything is permissible for me.

**Deeper truth:** But not everything is beneficial.

**Truth:** Everything is permissible for me.

**Deeper truth:** But I will not be mastered by anything.

**Truth:** Food for the stomach and the stomach for food.

**Deeper truth:** But God will destroy them both.

How do you relate these deeper truths to your struggles with food?

- What sacrifice have you made that you could insert in the spaces below to personalize the truth of the apostle Paul's statement in Philippians 3? (You may wish to refer back to your responses in question 2 above).

Yes, _____ is worthless when compared with the infinite value of knowing Christ Jesus my Lord. For his sake I have discarded _____, counting it all garbage, so that I could gain Christ and become one with him. (Philippians 3:7 – 9a NLT)

I can make the choice to identify my shortcomings and, instead of using them against myself, hand them over to Jesus and let Him chisel my rough places. The grace-filled way Jesus chisels is so vastly different than the way I beat on myself. My beatings are full of exaggerated lies that defeat. His chiseling is full of truth that sets me free.

*Made to Crave*, page 184

4. What is the one shortcoming you struggle with to the point of repeatedly beating yourself up — by comparing yourself to others, calling yourself names, exaggerating your failures?

If you feel ready to surrender your shortcoming, use the space below to write a brief prayer. Ask the Lord for His grace-filled chiseling to do its work in your life. Surrender your club of self-condemnation and ask Him to keep it from you. Submit yourself to His love and care.

With God, our intentional sacrifices become more than just sacrifices; they become expressions of love and trust that draw us closer to Him. It's a kind of "losing" strategy in which our losses pale in comparison to our gains — the riches of intimacy with Christ and increased strength to pursue holiness in every aspect of our lives.

● DAY 5: **Read and Reflect**

Read chapter 19 of *Made to Crave*. If you want to dig a little deeper, use a notepad or journal to work through the personal reflection questions at the end of the chapter. Use the space below to note any insights or questions you want to bring to the next group session.

● DAY 6: **Live as an Overcomer**

Hope is an essential companion on the journey to lifelong healthy eating. In order to sustain our victories, we have to believe that, with God's help, it is possible to overcome our past defeats and failures. It is possible to draw closer to Christ through our struggles with food. It is possible to make healthy, holiness-producing choices every day. And it is possible to live as an overcomer — a Jesus girl who craves God, not food.

> Yes, I've lost pounds and inches. But not being weighted down mentally and spiritually by the constant feeling of defeat is the real victory.
>
> *Made to Crave*, page 187

1. A significant part of the *Made to Crave* journey is about moving from being weighted down by failure and defeat to embracing empowerment and hope. How much empowerment and hope did you feel at the

beginning of this study? How much empowerment and hope do you feel right now? Fill in the two columns below to indicate your response.

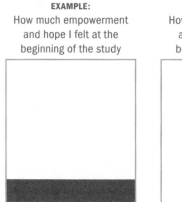

**EXAMPLE:**
How much empowerment and hope I felt at the beginning of the study

How much empowerment and hope I felt at the beginning of the study

How much empowerment and hope I feel right now

- If you were to show someone your columns, how would you explain them?

- Between the beginning of the study and now, how would you describe the difference, if any, in your *want-to*—your spiritual and mental motivation to make lasting changes?

2. Psalm 107 describes a time when God's people suffered from their rebellious choices and how God then saved them when they cried out to Him. Read the passage and then use the phrases below to reflect on the ways the psalmist's words provide a framework for your own experiences.

   Some became fools through their rebellious ways and suffered affliction because of their iniquities. They loathed all food and drew near the gates of death. Then they cried to the LORD in their trouble, and he saved them from their distress. (Psalm 107:17–19)

Some of my foolish habits with food have been . . .

   Examples: *Eating in secret, eating for comfort or stress relief*

Some of my rebellious ways with food have been . . .

Examples: *Intentionally choosing unhealthy options, eating unrealistic portions, refusing to acknowledge my need to address this issue*


Afflictions I've suffered—physically, emotionally, spiritually—because of food include . . .

Examples: *High cholesterol levels, feelings of guilt, feeling spiritually defeated*


How I have cried out to God for help with food . . .

Examples: *Prayers for strength to resist temptation, using healthy go-to scripts based on God's Word, remembering I am a lavishly loved child of God*


How I have experienced God's help in my distress over food . . .

Examples: *Increased strength to make healthy choices every day, a sense of peace about food, new habits I can sustain for a lifetime*


There's a reward for pressing through our struggles all the way to absolute victory. Virtually everyone who overcomes will tell you their victory is the sum total of a whole lot of hard decisions, sacrificial decisions, that they made choice by choice, day by day. Yes, knowing a reward awaits us is crucial. And how absolutely tickled I am to know that the reward for overcomers is that they are given the right to *eat*!

*Made to Crave,* 191

3. Revelation was written at a time when Christians were beginning to be persecuted for refusing to worship Caesar, the Roman emperor. The author of Revelation, traditionally believed to be the apostle John, writes to encourage his readers to persevere through their trials.

> He who has an ear, let him hear what the Spirit says to the churches. To him who overcomes, I will give the right to eat from the tree of life, which is in the paradise of God. (Revelation 2:7)

- It's unlikely we'll face literal persecution for our food choices, but food can become the equivalent of emperor worship—a false idol—in our lives if we rely on it and crave it more than we rely on and crave God. In the Revelation passage, the first thing the apostle John encourages his vulnerable readers to do is to listen to what the Holy Spirit is saying. What role does the Holy Spirit play in your choices when you are vulnerable to temptations with food?

As you continue your healthy eating journey, how might you make listening to the Holy Spirit an intentional and routine part of your healthy eating efforts?

- In granting overcomers the right to eat from the tree of life, God promises complete restoration of the relationship that was broken when sin entered the Garden of Eden.* It is a vision of nourishing, intimate, and eternal connection with God. In what way has your connection with God been nourished and deepened by the things you've overcome in your struggles with food?

Dare to set your toes firmly on the pathway of victory you are meant to be on. Whether we're on the path toward victory or defeat is determined by the very next choice we make. Not the choices from yesterday. Not the choices five minutes ago.

The next choice. Our very next choice. May it be that of an overcomer. An overcomer made to crave God alone.

*Made to Crave*, page 192

---

* "The thought takes up that of Genesis 3, where after eating of the tree of the knowledge of good and evil, man is barred from the tree of life. Those who overcome the trials and temptations of this world ... are promised not only restoration of what Adam lost but access to life in a way which Adam never had." "Paradise," by Hans Bietenhard, *New International Dictionary of New Testament Theology*, vol. 2, Colin Brown, gen. ed. (Grand Rapids: Zondervan, 1976, 1986), 762.

4. Pause to reflect on what you've learned and experienced throughout this study. As a refresher, briefly review your notes and responses in the previous group sessions and personal Bible studies. For each session, use the spaces provided below to note the insight or experience that stands out most to you.

SESSION 1: From Deprivation to Empowerment (pages 11 – 30)

SESSION 2: From Desperation to Determination (pages 31 – 56)

> *I feel so good when I make healthy choices and see the results — not necessarily on the scale but on the inside of myself. I have changed. I am an overcomer!* —JANE D.

SESSION 3: From Guilt to Peace (pages 57   80)

SESSION 4: From Triggers to Truth (pages 81 – 104)

SESSION 5: From Permissible to Beneficial (pages 105 – 126)

SESSION 6: From Consumed to Courageous (pages 127 – 148)

Use the session notes from the previous page as the foundation for a prayer of gratitude. In the space below, express your thanks to God for what He's taught you and for how you've experienced His love and care throughout the study. Praise Him for all the evidence you've seen of His goodness. Commit your ongoing journey to Him and thank Him in advance for His continued faithfulness on your healthy eating adventure.

You are a Jesus girl who has set her toes on the path to victory. You are a Jesus girl who has learned to use her cravings as a prompt for prayer. You are a Jesus girl who has discovered the power of accountability and sharing the journey with others. You are a Jesus girl who knows how to lean into God's power rather than mere willpower. You are a Jesus girl who has put defeat behind her and peace before her. You are a Jesus girl who loves the irony of losing to gain — you know the rewards are worth it. You are a Jesus girl who has an ear for the Holy Spirit and a heart starved for holiness. You are a Jesus girl who knows who she is — a lavishly loved child of God. And you are a Jesus girl who knows she was created to crave God, not food.

> *"Are your ears awake? Listen. Listen to the Wind Words, the Spirit blowing through the churches. I'm about to call each conqueror to dinner. I'm spreading a banquet of Tree-of-Life fruit, a supper plucked from God's orchard."*
> —REVELATION 2:7 MSG

# Moving the Mountain

## Group Discussion: *The Week in Review* (5 MINUTES)

If your group meets for two hours, allow **20 MINUTES** for this discussion.

Welcome to the Bonus Session of *Made to Crave*. A key part of this healthy eating adventure is sharing your journey with each other. Before watching the video, take some time to talk about your experiences since the last meeting. For example:

- What insights did you discover in the Bible studies or the *Made to Crave* chapters you read?

- What challenges or victories did you experience in applying what you learned in the last session?

- What questions would you like to ask the other members of your group?

## Video: *Moving the Mountain* (12 MINUTES)

As you watch the video, use the outline below to follow along or to take notes on anything that stands out to you.

### Notes

Mark's prayer: "Lord Jesus, there's so much to learn. Will you move the mountain of knowledge into my head?"

Mark's dad, Art, came home with a load of rocks in his truck. He said, "Mark, you're gonna need to move these rocks." The rocks were big, heavy, and hard to hold. It took Mark several hours.

"I tell you the truth, if you have faith as small as a mustard seed, you can say to this mountain, 'Move from here to there' and it will move. Nothing will be impossible for you." (Matthew 17:20 – 21)

Art explained to Mark: "God is helping you to move the mountain of knowledge into your head one lesson at a time. Sometimes our journeys in life aren't so much about witnessing the miracle of the mountain moving as they are about experiencing God taking our hand and walking through the journey with us."

Reviewing the *Made to Crave* journey — and all the rocks we've moved.

- SESSION 1: From Deprivation to Empowerment

- SESSION 2: From Desperation to Determination

- SESSION 3: From Guilt to Peace

- SESSION 4: From Triggers to Truth

- SESSION 5: From Permissible to Beneficial

- SESSION 6: From Consumed to Courageous

Make the choice to be courageous and you will see your mountain move.

## Group Discussion: *Moving the Mountain* (10 MINUTES)

If your group meets for two hours, allow **15 MINUTES** for this discussion.

Take a few minutes to talk about what you just watched.

1. What part of the teaching had the most impact on you?

2. In what ways do you relate Mark's struggles and frustrations to your struggles and frustrations with food and weight loss?

## Individual Activity: *My Rocks* (9 MINUTES)

Complete this activity on your own.

1. As you reflect on what you've learned and experienced throughout *Made to Crave*, what challenges have you overcome? In other words, what "rocks" would you say you've moved? Briefly note each one by writing it on one of the rocks below.

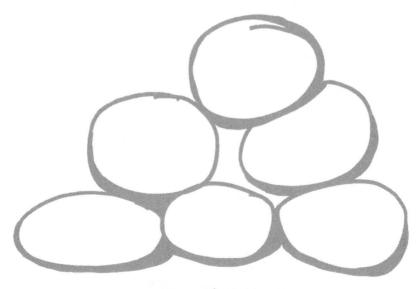

**THE ROCKS I'VE MOVED SO FAR**

2. When you think about maintaining your victories in the future, what challenges do you think you might face? In other words, what "rocks" do you think you might have to move or keep moving to stay on a healthy path? Briefly note each one by writing it on one of the rocks below.

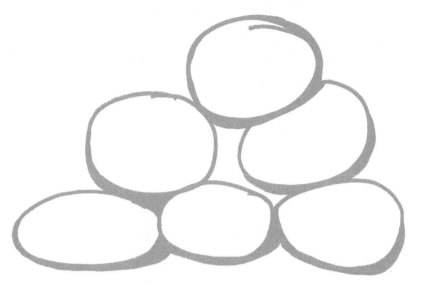

**THE ROCKS I WILL NEED TO MOVE OR KEEP MOVING TO STAY ON A HEALTHY PATH**

## Group Discussion: *My Rocks* (22 MINUTES)

If your group meets for two hours, allow 30 MINUTES for this discussion.

1. What rocks have you already moved?

2. Did anything surprise you about the rocks you've already moved? For example, were any of them things you didn't think were possible when you attended the first session?

3. Celebrate your accomplishment! A round of applause and a few hoots and hallelujahs is a good start. Then take a moment to come up with three or four additional ways to celebrate. Since many of us are used to celebrating with food, this is an important discussion — how might you celebrate your accomplishments without using food as a reward?

4. What rocks will you need to move or keep moving to stay on a healthy path?

5. What resources and support will you need to sustain you as you continue your healthy eating journey?

## Partner Activity and Group Discussion: *Mountain-Moving Faith*
(30 MINUTES)

If your group meets for two hours, use this activity and discussion as part of your meeting. Allow 30 minutes total — 10 minutes for the partner activity and 20 minutes for the group discussion.

### Partner Activity (10 MINUTES)

Pair up with one other person. Read Matthew 17:14 – 21 and Mark 9:28 – 29 aloud, then discuss the questions that follow and note your observations in the space provided.

1. The disciples didn't appear to lack faith. In fact, they were so convinced they could heal the boy that they were surprised and confused when their efforts failed. What do Jesus' comments in Mark 9:28 – 29 reveal about the disciples' faith? If prayer is

evidence of reliance on God, what do you think the disciples were relying on when they failed to heal the boy?

2. For a fresh perspective on Jesus' description of mountain-moving faith, read this passage aloud from *The Message*:

> When the disciples had Jesus off to themselves, they asked, "Why couldn't we throw it out?" "Because you're not yet taking God seriously," said Jesus. "The simple truth is that if you had a mere kernel of faith, a poppy seed, say, you would tell this mountain, 'Move!' and it would move. There is nothing you wouldn't be able to tackle." (Matthew 17:19–20 MSG)

Jesus appears to be commenting on the *quality* of the disciples' faith as much as the *quantity* of it. And He challenges them to believe that impossible things are possible with even the smallest portion of a faith that takes God seriously. How would you describe the difference between faith like the disciples had and mountain-moving faith?

## Group Discussion (20 MINUTES)

1. The disciples thought they were acting in faith, but they were still not able to heal the boy. In what ways would you say their faith was incomplete?

2. What insights do you gain from the disciples' experience that you can apply to your own life? How might these insights help you in your efforts to eat healthier and sustain long-term changes?

3. What would you say distinguishes mere faith from mountain-moving faith?

4. In what ways have you experienced mountain-moving faith on your *Made to Crave* journey? How might you continue to exercise mountain-moving faith — a faith that takes God seriously — in your healthy eating efforts?

**Individual Activity:** *What I Want to Remember* (2 MINUTES)

Complete this activity on your own.

1. Briefly review the outline and any notes you took.

2. In the space below, write down the most significant thing you gained in this session — from the teaching, activities, or discussions.

   *What I want to remember from this session ...*

## Closing Prayer

Close your time together with prayer.

# About Lysa TerKeurst

Lysa TerKeurst is a wife to Art and mom to five priority blessings named Jackson, Mark, Hope, Ashley, and Brooke. The author of more than a dozen books, she has been featured on *Focus on the Family*, *Good Morning America*, the *Oprah Winfrey Show*, and in *O Magazine*. Her greatest passion is inspiring women to say yes to God and take part in the awesome adventure He has designed every soul to live. While she is the cofounder of Proverbs 31 Ministries, to those who know her best she is simply a car-pooling mom who loves her family, loves Jesus passionately, and struggles like the rest of us with laundry, junk drawers, and cellulite.

WEBSITE: If you enjoyed this book by Lysa, you'll love all the additional resources found at *www.MadetoCrave.org*.

BLOG: Dialog with Lysa through her daily blog, see pictures of her family, and follow her speaking schedule. She'd love to meet you at an event in your area! *www.LysaTerKeurst.com*.

# A Gift Just for You

Get this free colorful magnet to keep you inspired and on track. The only charge is $1.00 for shipping and handling. To order, email: *Resources@Proverbs31.org* and put "Made to Crave Magnet" in the subject line. Bulk orders for Bible studies and small groups are also available with special shipping rates.

To download other free inspirational sayings, be sure to visit *www.MadetoCrave.org*, where you'll find many additional resources.

## About Proverbs 31 Ministries

If you were inspired by *Made to Crave* and yearn to deepen your own personal relationship with Jesus Christ, I encourage you to connect with Proverbs 31 Ministries. Proverbs 31 Ministries exists to be a trusted friend who will take you by the hand and walk by your side, leading you one step closer to the heart of God through:

- *Encouragement for Today*, free online daily devotions
- The *P31 Woman* monthly magazine
- Daily radio program

To learn more about Proverbs 31 Ministries, contact Holly Good (*Holly@Proverbs31.org*), or visit *www.Proverbs31.org*.

### Proverbs 31 Ministries
616-G Matthews-Mint Hill Road
Matthews, NC 28105
*www.Proverbs31.org*

# Becoming More Than a Good Bible Study Girl DVD Curriculum

## Living the Faith after Bible Class Is Over

*Lysa TerKeurst, President of Proverbs 31 Ministries*

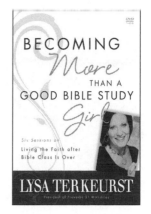

"I really want to know God, personally and intimately."

Those words of speaker, award-winning author, and popular blogger Lysa TerKeurst mirror the feelings of countless women. They're tired of just going through the motions of being a Christian: Go to church. Pray. Be nice. That spiritual to-do list just doesn't cut it. But what does? How can ordinary, busy moms, wives, and workers step out of the drudgery of religious duty to experience a living, moment-by-moment, deeply intimate relationship with God?

In six small group DVD sessions designed for use with the *Becoming More Than a Good Bible Study Girl Participant's Guide*, Lysa shows women how they can transform their walk with God from lackluster theory to vibrant reality. The *Becoming More Than a Bible Study Girl* DVD curriculum guides participants on an incredible, tremendously rewarding journey on which they will discover how to:

- Build personal, two-way conversations with God.
- Study the Bible and experience life-change for themselves.
- Cultivate greater authenticity and depth in their relationships.
- Make disappointments work for them, not against them.
- Find incredible joy as they live out their faith in everyday circumstances.

*Available in stores and online!*

## Share Your Thoughts

**With the Author:** Your comments will be forwarded to the author when you send them to *zauthor@zondervan.com*.

**With Zondervan:** Submit your review of this book by writing to *zreview@zondervan.com*.

## Free Online Resources at
## www.zondervan.com

**Zondervan AuthorTracker:** Be notified whenever your favorite authors publish new books, go on tour, or post an update about what's happening in their lives at www.zondervan.com/authortracker.

**Daily Bible Verses and Devotions:** Enrich your life with daily Bible verses or devotions that help you start every morning focused on God. Visit www.zondervan.com/newsletters.

**Free Email Publications:** Sign up for newsletters on Christian living, academic resources, church ministry, fiction, children's resources, and more. Visit www.zondervan.com/newsletters.

**Zondervan Bible Search:** Find and compare Bible passages in a variety of translations at www.zondervanbiblesearch.com.

**Other Benefits:** Register yourself to receive online benefits like coupons and special offers, or to participate in research.

**ZONDERVAN**®

**ZONDERVAN**.com/
**AUTHORTRACKER**
*follow your favorite authors*